ATOMIC HABITS

Let's Change your Atomic Habits!
A Full Simple Guide to Break your
Bad Routines and learn New
Good Ones

Author: **Mark Clear**

Table Of Contents

Chapter 1

Introduction to Habits

What's The Habit?

In order to change the habit, we need to know what we're dealing with!

Habits are routine behaviors that are performed on a regular basis. These are patterns of behavior that occur frequently and often lose consciousness through repeated learning. Many of them are unconscious because we don't even realize we're doing it.

The Merriam-Webster online dictionary defines the following habits:

1. The behavior obtained is almost or completely involuntary

2. The nature or characteristics of the person's thoughts and emotions

3. Steady trend or customary behavior

4. Behavioral patterns obtained through repeated repetition or physiological exposure manifested in regularity or improvement in performance

We can see that habits determine our personality, thoughts and feelings, as well as our "natural" behavior. We can also see that habits are almost involuntary or wholly repetitive and often become "better" (efficiency).

Habits can also be seen as the link between motivation and response. It is a spiritual link between the release of ideas or events (stimuli) and our response (response) to the release of events. The frequency of this communication usually affects all subsequent decisions and actions. If this link is repeated repeatedly, it will always remain unless we consciously intervene to change it.

For example, excessive stimulation can be stressful. Stress can be physical, emotional, or spiritual, due to factors such as limited nutrition, fatigue, fighting, daily work and even negative thoughts. Diet can be a scientific response to this stress. Over time, this combination becomes so strong that we respond to stress automatically or naturally during the diet. In psychology, this is called the classical case, as Pavlovian shows. Dogs learn to associate the sound with food, and when they hear sound, they always add salt, whether they have food or not.

In order to break down this negative behavior and ultimately eliminate it, we must weaken the relationship between stimulus and response in order to "close it" at the end. Therefore, the technical name "extinction" refers to this word.

Habits are the rituals and behaviors that we automate. It allows us to do important things, like brushing our teeth, bathing, dressing and walking the same way every day without thinking. Our unconscious habits allow brain resources to perform other more complex tasks, such as solving problems or choosing dinner.

We all usually have hundreds of thousands of habits a day. These habits can be divided into three categories. The first group includes habits that we will never notice, because they have always been part of our lives, such as shoelaces or brushing our teeth. Second, there are some habits useful to us, and we will work hard - for example, exercise, a good diet or adequate sleep. The latter group includes harmful habits such as smoking, indecision or excessive use. But where are these habits maintained? Let me introduce Charles Duhigg as well as his book "The Power of Habits" in this book.

Charles Duhigg is a New York Times journalist and author of The Power of Habit: Why We Do What We Do in Life and Business. He has held hundreds of interviews with scientists, research and research organized into organizations and read all he could to write this book on habits. so, we trust him.

To go into more detail about habits, we first exclude the possibility that we can rely on the will indefinitely.

Addiction and habits:

Habits can also be addictive.

Some people believe that the term addiction should be reserved to describe physical addiction to chemicals such as alcohol and drugs.

Other addictions include many compulsive behaviors such as playing, eating, shopping, playing video games, working and using the Internet. This addiction is often referred to as "mental addiction" and may also be associated with physical addiction.

A habit is a form of simple learning - behavior changes with experience. It is defined as "an automatic response to a particular situation, usually resulting from repetition and learning." When behavior develops to a very automatic degree, it is usually said. Usually we don't need our attention.

The term habit is strictly applied to the motor response, but is usually applied to the way of thinking and may correct the above settings.

Habits play an important role in our daily lives. We all have different habits. They are part of our lives.

Habits can be good or bad. Hardworking, writing, reading, regular exercise, meditation, etc. are examples of good habits. Alcohol abuse, drug use, drowsiness, procrastination, lying, dishonesty, theft, fraud, and escape are all examples of bad habits.

Main Basis of Habit Formation:

The composition of the habit can be explained in two ways: physical and psychological.

The physiological basis is related to the nervous system. When an action is repeated several times, it produces a clear nervous connection and leads to the pathway. This allows for the smooth transfer of nerve energy, possibly from the sensor to the engine.

According to Hal, when stimulation is repeated and the response is triggered, the connection is improved. Finally, there is usually a learning organization or nervous system.

The psychological habit of explaining habit is the acquired trait. According to these theories, any educational process or experience of the person will be stored. When this learning experience is repeated, it is still strongly rooted. Maintaining this ability helps to strengthen this ability and develop habits.

Types of Habits:

Depending on the type of activity, habits are divided into three types.

1. Leadership Behavior:

These habits indicate the muscle activity of the individual. These are habits associated with our body movements, such as standing, sitting, running, walking, training, maintaining a certain posture and so on.

2. Intellectual Habits:

These are the habits of psychological processes that require our intelligence, such as good observation, accurate perception, logical thinking, the use of thinking, before making decisions and verifying conclusions, etc.

3. Habits of Characters:

We express some personality in our habits. For example, helping the needy, trusting others, honesty, good speaking, arranging the time, working hard, keeping stylish clothes, etc., these habits express feelings and emotions. That's why we're also talking about emotional habits.

Effective Habit Formation Measures:

The famous American psychologist William James proposed the following general educational measures.

Start Well:

"A good start is half the battle" is a starting point. Therefore, we must start to learn habits. We need strong motivation and determination. We must not shake our minds. For example, a nursing student decides to start learning at a given time. He must start with the decision and do not hesitate on the first day.

Practice Regularly:

It is important to develop this new habit on a regular basis so that it becomes a daily habit in our lives. Delays or interruptions should be avoided as this will weaken our habits. For example, avoid disappointing excuses such as headaches, lack of interest, or lack of humor, and postpone work until later.

Choose an Enabling Environment:

Good public education also depends on an atmosphere of encouragement. Example: For students who want to work hard, there should be a group of hard-working students, not lazy colleagues who don't care about learning.

Don't Stop Until You Reach Your Goal:

Once you enter this habit, you should strengthen your habits. Therefore, it must continue until it is firmly rooted.

At the same time, we need to use new habits to discover more interest in ongoing practice. To this end, we can consider the positive impact of this new habit. For example: understand the subject, achieve good results, achieve good grades, do a good job, etc.

How the Habit is Formed?

When we do a new task for the first time, our brains work hard and process a lot of new information when they find their way. However, once we understand how the task works, the behavior begins to become automatic and the required intellectual activity is greatly reduced.

When you are in the parking lot for the first time in parallel or when you first confirm the shoelace, think about how much brain and attention you need. Compare this to your mental efforts in these activities.

"This brain process transforms a series of actions into automated programs called fragmentation, which is the origin of habit," Dossig writes. Expect dozens (or even hundreds) of behaviors every day. "

What is the Habit of Success?

The habits of success we have mentioned in personal learning are the social and emotional skills that students can achieve in academic and non-academic activities. The Emotional Social Learning (SEL) field is full of terms to describe the factors necessary for successful learning as well as traditional academic skills and content knowledge.

After a careful review of the current framework, Summit Learning adopted the "basic learning" framework developed by Dr. Brooke Stafford-Brizard (2016). The component framework integrates the most promising research for decades in socially emotional learning in a harmonious and comprehensive manner. Successful habits include skill development in five categories:

Health development (attachment, stress management, self-regulation);

Acceptance preparation (self-awareness, social awareness / interpersonal skills, leadership role)

Focus on school self and mindset (growth mentality, self-efficacy, belonging, the importance of school);

Perseverance (flexibility, freedom of choice, academic perseverance); and

Independence and sustainability (self-determination, curiosity, sense of purpose).

We believe that students will develop successful habits in the common relationship of the classroom. While other supervisors focus more on the interaction between students and their individual academic journeys, our learning framework "puts" into the classroom's social environment through a series of key relationships developed by students, teachers, colleagues and others. (Stafford Prizad, 2016). A successful framework for success is designed on the basis that basic skills are advanced skills, and skills are developed on the way of integrating cognitive, social and emotional skills.

The framework recognizes that children's lives are not always the same, and not everyone follows the same path. Teachers can help give advice on how to support students with trauma and other adverse conditions.

Research and Habits:

Scientists have discovered that the part of the brain called the basal ganglia plays a crucial role in creating and maintaining new habits. Therefore, scientists can understand why some people continue to do certain things after a serious brain injury. I always feel like I can find my way home without remembering where I'm going. Often, these people don't even know how or can still do something, but if the underlying node is intact, these old habits still exist. Recent research has also shown that our brains are solid, and we will continue to respect them even if we no longer benefit from them.

Researchers at Duke University have shown that more than 40% of our activities are determined by habits rather than choices. This shows that we can change our lives by eliminating bad habits and creating good habits. People who fully understand this can find great new ways to improve their lives.

Change the Habit:

The best way to change bad habits is to replace them with new ones. As you develop your habits, your brain creates new neurological pathways to enhance the application of these habits.

But why do people regain their old habits so often? In fact, the neural pathways created by the habits we develop will not disappear. These paths always exist when we need to go back and use the same path again. Of course, this can help us with many simple and automatic daily tasks such as walking, talking, running, and eating. Until we stand up and do it, we won't have to stop and think about what to do! (Of course, this applies to most of us, it is lucky and easy to do so.) Since these existing tracks have never been deleted, you can replace the current track with a new track.

Why Doesn't Willpower Work?

Speaking of the will, Charles said: "The will is not just a skill, it is a muscle like your muscles or your legs, and it gets tired as it works harder, which means less power for other tasks. "

Ever wonder why you want to order pizza if you work late? Or why not want to run after a day of hard work? Or why do you hate the idea of broccoli for dinner when eating a salad for lunch?

You have been using your will all day and you are no longer in it. I will dedicate you to another mystery - the best people who do things seem effortless do not use willpower.

How do Habits Work?

Charles said in the Power of Habits that most decisions we make every day can be considered well-considered decision-making products, but that's not the case. These are habits.

Habits are activities that you perform without having to decide at the beginning of each action whether you want to perform them. You don't have to think about how to do these things (most of the time), and sometimes you don't even realize you're doing something.

Do you think before brushing your teeth when you get up? Still wondering which subway to take if you've been in the same office

12

for three months? Are you afraid to press the accelerator pedal to change if you are an experienced driver? Take a moment to put on your running shoes in the morning while jogging for years?

No. But if you were to do all of these tasks willingly, you would take the time to decide to do them and see how you performed them (depending on the situation).

Habits automate your day and you will not even notice that you are negotiating automatically.

How Are Habits Formed?

I only wrote two years ago, but I have been blogging for two years now.

Driving does not feel like multitasking, even when we change, steer the bike, shift position between gas, brake and clutch and look back in the rear view mirror full of cars, sad state cars, horses and cows and more.

Once, these activities were not easy. Then we decided to do something - write, run, run. We started the task and the activity became part of our routine. While we feel it is worth doing these things, we do not think about whether or not we will do it. We do not go into their micromechanics. We make no choice. we only do the work - as if we were (almost) trained.

We make it a habit.

Listen to the conversation between two scientists about how the brain forms habits. I want to call these scientists Stephen and Kalam.

Stephen: Dude, have you heard of this thing called basic ganglions? Many scientific friends explore this part of the brain.

Kalam: Yes. This is the part of the brain that stores patterns. But what about the prefrontal cortex? Does she no longer make decisions?

Stephen: The prefrontal cortex has always been lazy. When it's up to her to decide, she makes a habit of doing everything we do. When Mrs. Cortex sees a trend, she hands over control to Mr. Ganglia. The ganglia detect patterns and repeat them immediately. Meanwhile, the cortex is lazy. Once the ganglia have repeated the pattern loop, Cortex takes over.

Kalam: Oh, here, there! But what is a model for brains? What does habit mean?

The Loop of Habits:

The brain resembles a circular habit pattern. To understand how habits work, we need to know how this course works.

Habits include the signal - signal or trigger, routine - the pattern we follow when we see the signal, and the reward - the reward we get when we follow the pattern.

The habit of brushing your teeth is as follows:

The key to brushing your teeth - you are very tired. Your usual style - brush your teeth. Your reward - a cold spot and a pleasant feeling of going to bed with clean teeth.

Rewards can also be called desires. In addition to the activation routine, the queue must activate one or more wishes to your liking by following the pattern.

If I ate chocolate after eating every day, the food was over. Fighting for sugar. His model is to eat Toblerone. Your bonus is so happy for your gentle age.

When you write at sunrise, your post is alert in the morning, your routine is written, and your reward is your satisfaction with writing the text.

We saw a signal, we did things, we got dessert, and we went out. When the brain detects the signal, the prefrontal cortex relaxes, and Stephen discusses it and speaks, and we follow the normal procedure.

Over time, the tracking, routine and reward cycle in our system becomes difficult. That's when we say that we have a habit - the answer is simple, because the desire is strong, and the convention is automatic.

But sometimes it is difficult to understand this desire. You may eat chocolate after a meal because you need sugar. But you may want to get more evening news within ten minutes, and you'll see if chocolate is slow to eat. Maybe you smoke coffee at four in the morning, do you think you like nicotine now? Smoking will not surprise you. 4 Catch a colleague instead of eating nicotine.

If we understand our requirements, we can change the usual curly hair and change our bad habits. As this series of habits develop, we will discuss these differences in desire.

Charles Duhigg's book The Power of Habits describes architectural habits as a three-step process:

First, there is an idea, a stimulus that tells your brain to switch to automatic mode and usage habits. Then there is a physical, psychological or emotional routine. Finally, there is a reward that can help your mind decide whether it is worth remembering this particular course...

Dushigg called it the usual session. This cycle becomes more automatic over time.

Habits are a more effective way for our brains.

Like everything, this is a balancing act. Our brains tend to make a normal autopilot. If we ignore the routine, or if we have a blind spot, we may not see bad habits that make us back off.

This is an ideal case for practicing consciousness.

Why Does Our Brain Create a Specific Habit?

We develop our habits because our brains don't want to think about the same thing every day. So, when he sees the pattern - he sees how we do the job several times - he remembers the model. The next time he sees the keyword - leading to the mode - he automatically activates the mode (usually), tilts back and rest.

When you develop your habits, your mind is no longer involved in making effective decisions. Charles said that nearly 40% of our daily activities are habits, not conscious choices.

When driving, we use the emotions (visual and acoustic) and driving habits (driving characteristics) that the brain remembers. At the same time, when we get into a meaningless flow, the brain or frontal cortex decides to slide into popcorn. However, once a horse-drawn car hits us from behind, the cerebral cortex pops up, throws popcorn into the air and starts working.

The brain's idea is simple - you need me, and I'll be there. Otherwise, I have to be because I work hard.

But why doesn't the brain always work?

Importance of Habits:

Imagine everything from morning to late night, from newspapers to brushing your teeth at night.

Do you remember that you did not do your daily work that day but delivered a speech or visited another office? Then you leave the rest area because you have to do other things. There does not seem to be a normal phenomenon.

If we decide what to expect every day, the same unpleasant feeling will bother us all day. At the same time, even if we complete the task day after day, we are finally exhausted.

"Without this habit, our brains will be closed and flooded because of the trifles of everyday life," Charles said. "People with injuries or illnesses in their basic faith are often paralyzed. For example, opening the door or deciding on eating and losing. Basic that ignores petty details, for example, a study found that patients with basal ganglia lesions are unable to recognize facial expressions, including anxiety and disgust because they do not know that they should care without losing our basic nodes. Face we can make hundreds Habits every day. "

Without habit, fatigue in everyday life will kill us. Habits make our lives more automated. The importance of habits is that they prevent the effort of one activity (and any activity).

More disciplined behavior is also practiced through habits. (Also read why learning is more important than results.)

Organizations (such as McDonald's, Pepsi, Starbucks), people working in harsh environments and in need of discipline (such as military personnel), who participate in international competitions (such as football players or Olympic swimmers) should be properly trained. And do what they have to do, even if they don't have time to make a decision.

We see that these people are fighting the enemy on the battlefield, on the pitch, or in the tensest situations, and they can't breathe every day to play bullets or work with a smile every day without complaining. Although we believe these people do all the things they need, most of their orders, decisions and behaviors come from some of the habits they use to change their behavior around the clock, even in the most difficult situations. So. Unfavorable.

The little things we do every day - brush your teeth, let your partner sleep a good night, go to the office every morning, or run or practice yoga, except prepare food instead of ordering every night, take a positive attitude, smile outside the stranger - all this Make us our own, how we think, what we do and how we are happy and healthy.

"Water is the habit of living around us every day, in different options and intangible options - when we look at them, they become visible again. Water has dug a constantly growing channel that will regain its already existing path when it stops flowing," says Charles Dohig's book.

Change Habits with Mindfulness:

But what is a righteous thought? In the trust gap, Ross Harris defines them as:

Mindfulness is a state of mind, openness and concentration. When we are conscious, we can fully participate in what we do, without giving up useful ideas and acting effectively, without being under pressure from our emotions.

By showing anxiety and self-esteem, we can identify areas of life that we want to improve. Including changing our habits. We perform these automatic and unnecessary tasks. We are very wired. But by changing the rules, we can change the habit. Offers or triggers that lead to habits may remain the same. However, if we change the routine, we can change the habit.

For example, the keyword is boring, the routine is useless food, and the reward is feeling good or dissatisfied/boring about food. It is necessary to change habits, pay attention to signs of trouble, change the habit of listening to audio books every day, and the reward continues to feel good. Be aware of this hint and you should pay attention.

Agenda is a great way to identify keywords. Be sure to carry a small notebook with you. If you feel bored, please write them down. If you eat for no reason, please write it down. If there is a problem with your charges, please record every dollar you spend. Over time, you'll see the pattern appear.

These routines can lead to good habits or bad habits over time. Pay attention to what you do.

Self-Confidence is the Secret Weapon to Change Habits

Real change is usually the result of an open vision of the shortcomings. Or as Epictetus said: "Meditation is in good faith."

More than we admit, many of our days end in a state of imagination, and this inner monologue proves our good and bad things. If we make a mistake, our evolutionary instinct will interfere, and we will do everything we can to ignore the obvious: sometimes, everything is our fault.

These examples should look familiar: we get the necessary and useful comments from our manager or colleagues to make fun of them, but we don't recognize our stupidity. We realize that our effectiveness is declining, not curing the disease, but treating the symptoms, and putting them on the keyboard after an hour (then look for productive hackers because our workload is too heavy).

Over time, our daily work becomes the usual reaction, we can not stop thinking about what we do. What makes things more difficult is that many of us don't have the luxury of hiring managers (who are they doing?), which can help us identify our shortcomings and their impact.

Engaging before starting a standard response is one of the biggest challenges of our lives. Mindfulness arises when we run discipline and meditate mercilessly. Try it first and then explain that it is human nature. Trolling, stopping and admitting how difficult it is: "Wait, I'm right now because this person's opinion makes me just forget myself, and I'm anxious to say this. I'm an idiot, so I'll better!" Instead, we insist on explaining why.

Try it first and then explain that it is human nature.

According to Anthony K. Tajan, author of the Harvard Business Review, "... quality that goes beyond almost all business leaders, executives and executives. This quality is self-aware. Managers can do it. The best thing is to improve their efficiency and understand what drives them and their decisions."

Take a rest, and let us think about it, explain to us and acknowledge our stupidity, which is very important in promoting self-esteem. You must fight all confrontational and evolving behaviors - determined to protect your mind at all times - so don't spend your time in failed actions for the failed self, but stop and think, do better for yourself.

Self-knowledge is defined as knowledge of self-awareness; it is a starting point for reinventing ourselves, making more informed decisions, and controlling thoughts and feelings. We often blame external factors because they are the simplest justification for thinking about how we think and think, test our different opinions, and learn from mistakes.

The Roman philosopher Seneca once said: "For someone who does not know that he has done something wrong, there is no desire to correct it; he must recover."

Chapter 2

What are Bad Habits?

Habits for Under 25 Age Persons:

Have you ever seen a senior on your way? It is frustrating to see them repeat bad habits that are detrimental to their livelihoods. However, the saying is true: old habits die hard.

A Harvard study pointed out that "we are too often motivated by guilt, fear or regret, and the experts studying behavior change agree that lasting change is more likely" to be motivated and based on positive thinking. "

In other words, it is very difficult to change with age.

For this reason, it is important to develop successful habits early in life. If you start with these good habits now, you will be in good shape later. I encourage you to regard your habits as compound interest. Compound interest is an economic term that refers to the interest that is higher than the interest rate. If you invest with a specific interest rate over time, the interest rates will come to you.

If you deposit $ 1,000 into a 3% savings account, you can earn an additional $ 600 within five years without having to make any other deposits. Over the years, $ 1,000,000 can come from the same $ 1,000. In this case, the results are really based on the results.

If you develop good habits at a young age, you are ready for long-term success. I am reviewing more than 20 habits that you must have before the age of 25.

Travel Around The World:

It is important to see the world. Leaving your usual routine and comfort zone can extend your perspective. Travel can really help you understand and appreciate different people and cultures.

There are many online deals for those who want to travel cheaply. Travel with groups of friends to save costs. Consider using sites such as Airbnb for cheap hosting. The US dollar continues to evolve in many third countries, so you can have more than you think. See the various airlines and book tickets if they have really low prices. As long as you plan your excursions in advance, you can see the world in no time!

Learn How To Cook:

Everyone should eat. As the twenties, you need to know how to cook meals and make magic in the kitchen. Buying food quickly may seem cheap, but those dollars are rising fast. If you take two of the three meals a day, you can easily spend a lot of money that you will never see again. Instead, save your money and buy food for half the price.

When you join YouTube, you can find people who know how to cook your favorite dishes. Experiment and perfect these dishes. Soon you can prepare a gastronomic menu in no time. Decide if you want to take a cooking class this weekend to enrich your education and hobbies. Buy interesting cookbooks and learn how to cook a new dish every month. Your palace and wallet will thank you!

Don't be afraid to find "the one":

Yes, I know we live in a time when hormones are in full swing and beautiful people are everywhere. They are at an age where many people are looking for Mr. or Mrs. But don't spend your time searching for the perfect partner.

To prevent your emotions from being entangled, keep things clear. Don't spend a lot of time searching social media for a new date. It is best to focus on developing your mentality, career and other habits on this list.

If you talk about the opposite sex most of your time, you will have trouble engaging in a revealing conversation on another topic. Use this time to keep up to date with current events. Develop hobbies and choose what you like and dislike. Do not lose yourself by focusing on the following abdominal muscles or the curves that pass.

Know Different People:

It is wise to meet many people during your life. In addition, you don't have to go to bed with anyone to get to know him. instead of:

• Go to a good restaurant.

• Visit your local zoo or aquarium.

• Take part in a great concert.

• More dates.

If you go out with a few people at the same time, be sure to listen. You don't want the player to be called. Just learn to enjoy their company without having to become incredible or serious. By doing this, you can understand what you love and dislike. This will help you find a life partner (if you can). Consider different peoples and cultures. Love does not understand color.

Never Pursue Happiness

Don't accept what you think should happen. Also, don't look at what you see on social media and assume you're lucky. Learn to be satisfied with your current condition and develop a sense of satisfaction.

Of course, you may need to improve some aspects. Maybe your current situation is not optimal. However, although many people believe that happiness can be found in increased salary or partner's day or the next wedding day, this is not true. Although all these things are fun, they don't make you happy for long. Happiness is something you must work hard without having to follow it. Never trust someone who makes you happy or makes you happy.

Read:

There are many reasons to develop reading habits. Many of the most successful people in the world are enthusiastic readers who deliberately read books every day.

Remove busy excuses too. Now you can read audiobooks and read apps anytime, anywhere. Reading can improve your mind and vocabulary. Always develop your brain to meet the challenges of everyday reading.

Stop Bad Habits:

Just as it is important to maintain good and healthy habits, it is also important to get rid of bad habits. Smoking is a classic example. Smoking is definitely not good. By the age of 25, many young people liked to experience grass to understand its appearance. Don't give in to temptation. With the development of cigarette or weed addiction, it is really difficult. As an entry drug, this led to further drug trials.

In addition, bad habits like smoking have a greater impact on your health. It also drains your finances and destroys the opportunity to develop an active support system for your friends. Smoking, excessive diet and excessive money are all of your emotions. It is worth consulting or asking for help to eliminate the cause. Deliberately try to get rid of bad habits in different ways so you can continue to grow in a healthy way.

Drink Plenty of Water:

For optimal health, you need to consume about half of your body weight. Many people suffer from dehydration and lose consciousness. Many people try to solve the problem by drinking or drinking a caffeinated drink. However, the main cause is usually dehydration. Your body needs to detoxify the system and must rely on water to survive.

Imagine that the toilet was blocked after a whole day. You don't want to be there because it smells like there's something inside. The same applies to the body. Our body is extremely flexible, so we underestimate the power that can be used in our mistakes. However, their neglect will quickly lead to negative compound interest rates.

Exercise Every Day:

Make sure you exercise enough every day. Of course, as you age, your body will lose its effect unless you care about your body. If you have to sit at your desk all day, wake up early in the morning, then walk or walk. When you're away from home, you can recharge your body and wake up for a new day.

Proactive can also help you control your weight. The best way to lose weight is to combine diet and exercise.

Want to start practicing habits? Show:

Choose a weight-loss method: one pound per week of the final plan. Another good practice is weight lifting. For a long time after exercise, strength training burns calories. It is also ideal for strengthening the body, regulating stress hormones and improving heart health.

If you don't like mountain climbing or treadmills, try dancing, swimming or playing tennis. These options are fun and can move your body.

Start Eating Green Vegetables:

When I was young, most children hated the idea of eating sprouts of Brussels, spinach and kale. As an adult, you need to get rid of this situation. The food you hate in your childhood is the same as the food you need to keep your adult life.

There are countless ways to incorporate green food into your diet in a healthy and delicious way. Try green yogurt for breakfast. Put a cup of soy milk in the blender. Add bananas and some pineapples. Then add a small amount of organic cabbage. Mix for several minutes and you can enjoy a delicious milking.

Practice Part Control:

Yes, eating at leisure seems very attractive. However, managing an important part to maintain optimal health. Many people eat a lot and want to know why they want to add more! The American diet includes many of the majority. In restaurants like The Cheesecake Factory, a medium meal can easily feed three people.

It is important to know the weight and when to stop. If you have a piece of meat in your meal, the entire portion should not exceed the size of the palm. On the dish, vegetables should occupy half of the situation.

Look at some of the drinks you bought. If there are records of two servings in the pan, you can drink only half. Although candy is not good for health, most people still like a bag of gum. If the serving size is five small snacks, don't eat the whole bag at the same time.

Set Ambitious Goals, But Make Realistic Plans:

One of the most exciting aspects of youth is your potential. You have the ability to be whatever you want. All the dreams you have achieved in your childhood can achieve your goals.

Let your thoughts work freely when you want your ideas to be. Whether you're dreaming of becoming an astronaut, a professional singer or a doctor, it's time to sit down and plan to achieve that goal.

Think about what you're building. Make sure you try to fight yourself and others. When setting goals, consider starting small and starting to eliminate them. Soon, you will gain motivation, confidence and conquest. Soon, you can properly realize the dreams of your career.

Know That The Profession Is Not Everything:

Keep in mind that while it is important to develop your focus and dedication to achieving your goals, your career is not everything. You don't want to look back at life with regret.

Don't forget to spend time investing in family and social life. Don't forget to play. When your professional pressure is high, it's always good to do activities like family, friends and hobbies.

Mention the point:

• Always contact your family members and call them regularly.

• Adapt to relatives who may not be in town.

• Family visits are determined at least once a year.

• Build a healthy friendship and be with someone who loves you and knows you.

• Take your time to discover and invest your favorite hobbies.

• If you take the time to enjoy life, your successful career looks more satisfying.

Understanding Credibility Is Everything:

Your reputation is yours. A wise man once said, "Well, the world is a small city." This is truer than many people realize. It is important to prevent bridges from burning with people in the workplace. Even if your colleague or client is completely unfavorable to you, his unprofessional or hostile behavior will not allow you to enter a place that may damage your reputation.

A bad reputation is hard to explain. If someone doesn't think about you, they will remember, even if it's time to find someone who can do the work you can do. In business and life, you'll find that success depends on your knowledge. People are happy to build positive relationships and give them a good reputation.

Although movies and TV shows are ruthless, surrender and unclear, this does not translate into real reality. Of course, some people have reached the top of the well-known food chain - this is not a sustainable success at all.

Discover Your Enthusiasm

As the saying goes: "If you love what you do, you won't work again." Of course, some of your content may not be of interest to you. However, it is important to find a career you love and appreciate. After all, you spend most of your time in the profession. It's better not to take time off.

The best way is to make sure you live the life you want. This includes your business. Do not choose to work on the basis of salary or reputation. Because of these factors, I'm not happy if you're the only reason to work in a particular area.

No dollar sign or prize is worth your health and happiness. Find out what makes you shine from the inside and focus on it. If you can solve problems while pursuing your passion, real professional satisfaction can be achieved.

Get a Credit Card:

Once you make money and enter the business world, you begin to create credibility. At some point, you will buy a lot of goods, such as cars or houses, and if you do not have the balance, it is difficult to get a loan.

The key to using a credit card is to keep your credit card at a low price and monthly payment. Don't spend too much money on your credit card. Try not to use more than 30% of the available credit limit. This may be tempting, but when you look at your credit score and find it great, you'll like it.

Save For Your Future:

Compound interest is a powerful concept. The faster you save, the more money you earn. When you receive your salary, please make every effort to ensure payment first. If your financial profit margin is not high, you can try saving at least 5% of your salary.

Discipline in savings is important because there is always someone or something with you to withdraw money. At first, this seems very difficult. Therefore, it is important to adapt to it as soon as possible. The more you practice this habit the easier it is. When you begin to understand how to raise and raise money, you will be grateful and excited to continue this habit.

One of the tools I used to save is a robot consultant called Betterment, which simplifies the savings process by investing your money in a fund with a much higher return than the usual interest rate of 0.02%. Implementation of the bank savings account.

Maintain Your Monthly Budget:

Maintaining your monthly budget helps you achieve your financial goals better. This will also help you understand where your money is going. Keep the budget at zero. Every dollar you get must have a website.

When you create and maintain a budget, it's up to you to decide where to go. If you want to work out in the gym, think about it. If you want to invest more money in an investment fund, this is your decision. The budget is set at the beginning of each month. Check your performance at the end of each month and how you can improve yourself.

Do You Have A Contingency Plan?

When you are young, it is easy to think that you are invincible and nothing will happen. However, you need to consider an emergency. First, check out your car, auto and life insurance policies.

In the event of an accident, you need to make sure that your insurance company can cover these bills. Cancer is not out of respect for ageing. Even if you don't want to live your life, you don't know what to expect in the future if you have an incurable disease.

If you are sick and need leave, make sure your employer has good health insurance. Always have an emergency credit fund. If you don't have enough money, you can save $ 1000 on a fraudulent savings account. The Emergency Fund can save you a small amount of puncture, or you need to book a quick trip for funerals or unexpected situations.

Reduce Costs:

We live in a technological age and everything can be done easily by deleting the debit card. Most people don't have much money and you can easily spend money online with a single click. Because many companies simplify spending, it's important to understand your spending.

If you don't feel that your account is running out, it is easy to spend a lot of money. Take some time to get rid of the habit of spending a lot of money. When you feel that money is about to leave, you can easily make money.

Good Habits - Parents Should Teach to Children

Children are worried about their parents. Parents are always a reference point for children, and when they have problems, they will find children, and children will develop the habit as soon as possible. As we age, children follow their parents' behaviors, and parents are role models for children. Their wisdom and habits will inevitably spread to children. Therefore, it is important to teach children to distinguish between good habits and bad habits and choose the right habits.

Healthy Habits For Children:

It may be difficult to maintain good behaviors and healthy habits for your child. But be patient and guide them on the right path. The following elements can be considered healthy habits that children must develop:

Healthy Food:

Children tend to order more junk food, potatoes, candy, biscuits and chocolate. You should convince them that a healthy diet can have the same taste. You can also enjoy homemade versions of pasta, pasta, cakes, cookies and pizza.

In order to encourage children to develop this healthy habit, please follow a colorful path. The goal is to eat all the colors of the rainbow once a week, which means eating different colors when eating. This is not only beneficial to your health, but also ensures that children enjoy food. Parents should be a good example by eating regularly and evenly.

Sports Activities:

As a parent, it is a big mistake for children to watch TV on the couch. Don't let your child sit. Encourage them to start, walk, train, or send them to play. Plan a family event, enjoy, and bring children. If you are a potato bank, please tell your child that it is harmful to your health. Some health risks associated with sedentary lifestyles include:

• Obesity

• Sleep disturbance

• Pay attention to the bottom

• Emotional and social issues

Focus On Food Labels, Not Designers:

From age, especially during adolescence, your child will be interested in the label on the clothes. Tell your child about the most important poster for children - food label. Once you get used to the habit, encourage them to recognize the nutritional value of food.

Show them your favorite packaged foods and highlight important information on the food label. He developed a habit of reading these labels, analyzing the nutritional value, then determining its value. Encourage them to focus on important ingredients such as saturated and unsaturated fats, sugar, calories and carbohydrates. Their conscious efforts help to develop healthy habits and maintain the habit throughout their lives.

Dinner With Family:

Today, in our busy lives, the family and the elderly do not have much time. A busy life will prevent you from sitting with your child and listening to their stories and personal problems. Eating with your family is a priority. You can discuss a lot of things and share your opinions. This has a lasting effect on your child. Other benefits of eating together are:

• Children begin to feel comfortable and adapt to the family

• When you are older, children get good eating habits and avoid fast food.

• The tires have hardened

Moisturizing Health:

Drinking soft drinks is the most common feature of young children who follow the elderly. You need to guide your child and promote the importance of drinking water to avoid soft drinks. Just tell your child that water is healthy and helps to get rid of all kinds of diseases. Soft drinks are unhealthy because they contain a lot of sugar and calories, which can cause weight problems. Let them realize that water is an important resource and should take enough quantity to ensure adequate water. When your child realizes the importance of water to the body, they will definitely choose unhealthy soft drinks.

Clean Up The Mess:

It is necessary to teach hygiene in early childhood. Start by organizing things around your child well. If they used to see well, they would leave that way. When they're old enough, you can support them and give them time to clear the mess and put it right. By doing this regularly, they can learn quickly and work hard to organize their own things.

Responsible with Money:

When your child is responsible for shopping, you can tell them the value of the hard-earned money. You can save money by giving your child's pocket money or keeping a piggy bank from time to time. Give them a budget and encourage them to manage to spend and save money. This way, your child will learn the value of money and start saving.

Participation Is Important:

Children need to understand the value of certain things, learn to be grateful, and share them modestly with those who cannot afford them. Also teach them some dodgy things to share, such as emotions, feelings and stories. Children first learn to share with their families, including parents, grandparents, siblings, cousins and extended families, then share them with others. This common attitude will make him or her a better person.

Do Not Throw Public Places:

Teach your child a civilized and responsible citizen. Explain that garbage should not be dumped in public, but should be dumped in the next can. Help them develop this simple habit and ask them to follow it everywhere because it helps them improve. Develop a habit of not throwing garbage, and your child will follow your example. Always pay attention to garbage when throwing things. When you leave the house, you can take a small plastic bag with you and collect all the garbage (empty water, napkins, etc.). Take her home and throw her in the trash instead of on the table. The restaurant puts it all the way or outside the car window.

Courtesy:

Courtesy is a virtue that everyone admires. Teach your child to respect older or younger. Explain that even if they meet someone they don't like, they should be polite and divorced in a decent way. You should be calm and hospitable to everyone. These qualities will last a lifetime and will always be respected. Treat your child first with respect and you will find that they go into the habit. Be polite to girls.

Maintaining Justice:

Children are born pure and fair, and this distinction is part of the marital status. As a parent, all you have to do is make your child vulnerable to discrimination. Let them be fair and treat everyone equally, rich or poor, friends or enemies. You can encourage them to become friends with children of any religion or sect.

Avoid Damage To Animals Or Birds:

Children usually love animals and birds. Some people feel attracted, others are scared, others become defensive, others remain calm. They must understand that animals and birds are creatures that can communicate and be friendly in their own way. They must learn to distinguish between pests and harmless organisms. Advise them to stay away from pests and be friendly and friendly to them. You can tell them the same thing by watching documentaries and animal shows on TV.

Exercise Regularly:

Identify routine activities for you and your family so you can spend time together doing physical exercises such as running, jogging, swimming, exercising or doing yoga at home. In the long run, sports benefit the whole family. From the daily activities of the child, the child remains active, healthy and flexible. This helps create a healthy lifestyle for your child. Playing music can increase the excitement of exercise. The best way is to register a sport for your child. It will also teach you valuable lessons in life, most importantly sports.

Do Not Criticize Or Intimidate Anyone:

Cash can be adult or adult. At an early age, not everyone is smart enough to accept critical discourse. Parents need attention and guide their children to interact and act. Children should realize that criticism can harm others and should not tell them bad things. It is wrong and unacceptable to harass or harass people you hardly know. Turn your task into a serious discussion for your child's family members.

Tell The Truth:

Honesty is a very important virtue and should be applied to children from an early age. As a parent, you are a role model for your child. Their behavior and discourse have the greatest positive and negative impact on them. Always be straightforward, especially if you have children. In any case, they should have the motivation, to tell the truth.

Patience and Perseverance:

To be right, "patience is a virtue" because patience can live in peace. In today's stressful world, peace is what everyone wants. Give your child the opportunity to be patient and stay calm and peaceful.

Teach them to relax, calm, and wait for their pace or anything. Make sure your patience is profitable in all situations and can easily resolve any unfortunate situation. Encourage them to participate in activities such as gardening or cooking that do not immediately see results and require patience.

Thanksgiving:

Maintain a modest attitude towards children and teach them to be grateful to children of all sizes. Get the habit of waking up every morning and praying twice a day before bed. Follow it yourself and your child will learn from you

Brush Twice A Day:

Oral hygiene is very important and should be taken care of since early childhood. Develop good habits for a long time. Children often become lazy when brushing their teeth, but this daily task should not be easy. As a reward, you can sometimes treat her with her favorite sweets. Tell them the correct type of cleaning:

• Brush twice a day and twice a day

• Mouthwash after eating - this helps prevent bad breath and tooth decay

• Use the thread in time

• Clean the tongue with your tongue

Clean The Ears:

The ear is one of the most important organs in your body. Neglecting the ear can lead to nuisance or serious injury. It is especially important to keep your ears clean during childhood. Wash the outer ear with water daily and wipe with a dry cloth. As your child grows, you can teach them how to clean their ears.

Showers Per Day:

Bathing is a basic requirement and is recommended for people of all ages. This should occur within the first hour after waking up. On a hot summer day, your child can take two baths. Otherwise, your child should bathe after playing at home. The bathroom rejuvenates the skin, giving a fresh feeling and preparing to sleep day and night.

Children need to keep their hair clean. Scalp and hair often fade when traveling or playing outside. You need to wash your hair at least every two or three days. This protects them from lice, dandruff and excessive hair loss. Develop a habit of applying the oil regularly to the scalp before washing your hair. Also, make sure to use the comb to touch the scalp when combing. This improves blood flow to the scalp and promotes healthy hair growth.

Nails Should Be Short:

Children often tend to put their fingers in their mouths. Therefore, the nail should remain clean and free of dirt. As your child grows, you can tell them how to make your nails short and clean. You can explain to them that the nails will scratch or pass the mouth to make the bacteria sick, leading to bacteria entering the body. If your child is too old to attend school, please tell them about the importance of good health and good habits. In addition to the above healthy habits, school children should also pay attention to the following important habits:

"Please", "thank you" and "I'm sorry":

You need to teach your child three magic words "thank you", "thank you" and "sorry" so they can solve many problems easily. Society often appreciates and appreciates the use of these golden words. Your child will look polite and excited. Practice these words regularly with your child and they will use them a lot.

Helping Others:

Educate your children and make them useful. Show them the path of humility and generosity. Encourage them to help those in need as much as possible. Help your role help people, friends or strangers in front of your child and warn them against meeting strangers.

Active And Healthy Thinking:

Children are very sensitive and are easily discouraged by small things or things that do not fit their way. It is important to share and talk with them so that you know what the child is experiencing and what they think so that they are not discussed negatively. Avoid wrong compliments; instead, be sure to recognize their services and efforts in a timely manner. They can help them build trust by ensuring their children's abilities and unique qualities and ensuring that they are completely loved. Try to develop your thinking in a logical and practical way to be positive and think about it in the face of difficulties in your life.

Spend Time With Friends:

It is said that even at age, friendship at school will last longer. This is because the child has a pure idea. Have no selfish motives when making friends. At a very young age, friends play a very important role in a child's social development. Children learn life skills such as communication, social networking, collaboration, problem solving and teamwork with friends. As a teenager and adult, good friends are part of the child support system. Encourage your child to find friends, spend time, socialize and relax with them.

Do Not Miss Breakfast:

Breakfast is the most important meal of all ages. It is especially mandatory for children and an elementary school student because it stimulates brain function, metabolism and body and provides energy throughout the day. You can give your baby fiber products from breakfast cereals for breakfast as they reduce the risk of diabetes and heart disease. Getting used to breakfast will benefit him as an adult. Inform them about the harmful effects of breakfast bounce and repeat that eating in the morning increases the risk of obesity.

Table Manners:

At a certain age, children insist on eating on their own. Although they like spoons and forks, they can't do a good job and cause chaos. You need to be trained to eat properly. You can treat them like adults and show them the food label.

Regular Physical Exercise:

Children need to engage in activities such as sports, musical instruments, swimming or gymnastics to maintain physical activity. This habit promotes the development of children in all aspects. Children remain alert and alert; they learn to be strong and may continue to do so in adulthood. If your child doesn't want to exercise or is afraid to exercise, continue to encourage them to try new things and prevent them from doing other activities. Sooner or later, they will find challenges, entertainment and entertainment.

Reading Every Day:

The best way to practice reading with your child is to include them in the game and at the time of the child's sleep. Choose to have your child read interesting books. Develop their daily habits because they help build children's confidence in themselves and improve their reading skills and develop their imagination, vocabulary and creativity. This helps to improve relationships and communication with parents.

Time Value:

We know the term "time is money" and we know the value of time and money. Children need to learn how to spend their time properly, punctuality, follow daily schedules and follow-up schedules. Help them understand that they must go to school on time because they may be punished for not attending classes on time. As a family, you can participate in various events or gatherings. Be sure to communicate at any time or at any time, and as the child grows, they will remember the same habits.

Sleep On Time:

Sleep is essential for children's growth and development. You need to introduce your child to the habit of waking up early and waking up when he is young. Children attending school should be active every day and need adequate sleep. During sleep, the body retains all the energy lost during the day. By going to bed early, your child can rest completely and feel healthy and active the next day.

• Go to bed early, wake up early, and let the baby sleep early. Your child feels safe and sleeps when you are nearby

• Go to bed at the same time every day. This helps to determine the pattern of children and allow them to learn to sleep alone

• Do not let your baby sleep longer than necessary. Children can take a nap if necessary.

Acceptance Failed:

Children often feel uncomfortable when they fail. As parents, it is your responsibility to support and motivate them to respond to failure in a positive way and do their best next time. You need to understand the ups and downs of life and understand that not all failures are permanent. This is not always about winning or losing. The energy you put and the progress you make are also important.

Voltage:

Get your child out of the importance of hard work. Whether it's reading, writing or constructive work, you should develop a habit of doing everything. They must understand that happiness alone does not encourage success. This requires hard determination and hard work. You can set an example for your children and show how difficult your job is.

Do Not Smoke, Drink or Use Drugs:

Habits such as drinking, smoking and drug use depend largely on family background and education. Make sure you are fully involved in your child's life, understand their shortcomings and support them at all stages because neglect and lack of communication make them vulnerable to external influences. You need to educate your child about these bad habits and teach them to avoid all costs. He also warned the children of the impact of their peers. As a parent, you can help yourself by not smoking or smoking.

You can teach your child's discipline, but whether or not your child uses it depends on how you teach your child in a parent's way in your daily life. He showed them the right way and encouraged them to definitely stick and praise.

Chapter 3

What are Bad Habits?

Break 10 bad habits

They are your total habits. If bad habits lead you, it will seriously hinder your success. The problem is that bad habits spread slowly so you don't even notice the damage they cause.

"The usual strings are too light to feel too heavy to break." - Warren Buffett

Breaking bad habits requires restraint - a lot of them. Studies have shown that this is useful because restraint can have a significant impact on success. University of Pennsylvania psychologists Angela Duckworth and Martin Seligman have researched the degree of self-monitoring of IQ and college students. Four years later, students scored and found that self-control was twice as important as IQ to achieve a high GPA.

The restraint required to develop good habits (and stop bad habits) can also be a basis for building good professional ethics and high productivity. Self-control is like a muscle, and you should train him to exercise. Practice reducing self-control by developing the following bad habits:

Use Your Phone, Tablet Or Computer In Bed:

What is important is that most people do not even realize that it affects their sleep and productivity. Blue short-wave lamps play an important role in your mood, energy levels and sleep quality. In the morning, the sun contains a lot of this blue light. When your eyes touch it directly, the blue light stops producing melatonin (hypnotic hormone) and feels more alert. In the afternoon, the sun loses blue light, which causes your body to produce melatonin and make you feel sleepy. At night, your brain does not expect exposure to blue light, so it is very sensitive to it.

In the evening, most of our favorite devices - laptops, tablets and mobile phones - will emit a bright, short-wave blue light directly on your face. When you agree, this exposure can affect melatonin production, your ability to sleep, and your sleep quality. As we all know, lack of sleep can have serious consequences. The best way is to avoid using these devices after dinner (most people watch TV as long as they are away from the device).

Motivation Online:

It takes 15 minutes to fully focus on the task. When you're done, you'll be in a thriving state, a process that increases productivity. Studies have shown that people in liquid form are five times more productive than others. No need to work, itch, news, Facebook, sports score or everything you lose. This means that you must stay focused for another 15 minutes to return to the power state. Always click on your business and go out, you can lose energy all day long.

Check The Phone During The Call:

Nothing prevents people from sending text messages during conversations and even during a quick tour of your phone. When you start a conversation, you put all your energy into the conversation. If you participate, the conversation will be more interesting and effective.

Use Multiple Messages:

Multiple reports are a nightmare to increase productivity. Research shows that moving your phone and sending emails can reduce productivity whenever you focus. If you receive a notification each time you receive a message on your phone or receive an email in your inbox, it may not work. Instead of working to your liking, you collect and check all emails and text at specific times (for example, replying to an email every hour). This is an effective method.

If you say "no", please say "yes":

A study by the University of California at San Francisco suggests that the more likely you are to experience stress, fatigue or even restraint, the harder it will be to refuse it. Saying no to many people is actually a big challenge. The word "no" is a strong word, do not worry. When it comes time to say no, sensible people avoid using phrases like "I don't think I can't do it" or "I'm not sure." If you decline a new commitment, your existing obligations will be honored and you will have the opportunity to meet them successfully. Remember, nothing is self-control behavior that can improve control of yourself in the future by preventing the negative effects of excessive participation.

Think of the Poison:

There will always be toxins that have a chance to enter the skin and stay there. When you think of a colleague or someone boiling blood, you are grateful to others in your life. There are a lot of people who should pay attention to you, and the last thing you have to do is think of people or people who don't care.

Perform Various Tasks During The Meeting:

Don't focus on anything, especially in meetings. If the meeting is not worth your attention, you do not need to attend the meeting. If the meeting deserves your attention, please do everything possible. Multitasking during a meeting can hurt you and give you the impression that you think you're more important than anyone else.

Applause:

The club is happy with the tragedies of others. It may be fun to start looking at someone else's personal or professional mistakes, but over time, it becomes very stressful and you feel sick and hurt others. There are so many positive things and a lot of interesting people to learn a lot that wastes your time talking about the pain of others.

"Big men discuss ideas, general ideas about events, and young people discuss people." Eleanor Roosevelt

Wait Until You Know You've Succeeded:

Most writers spend countless hours modifying their characters and movements, even page after page, knowing they won't be included in the book. They do this because they know that developing ideas takes time. We tend to stop at first because we know that our ideas are not perfect and that what we produce may not be true. But how can you do that much if you don't start from scratch and don't give your ideas time to develop? Author Judy Piccolt summarizes the importance of perfect perfection: "You can edit damaged pages, but you can't edit blank pages."

Compare Yourself to Others:

When you feel happy and satisfied when you compare with others, you will no longer be the owner of your happiness. If you are satisfied with what you do, don't be attracted to the opinions or results of others. Although it is impossible to dispel your perceptions of others, you don't have to compare yourself with others, but you can always keep the axes' minds united. This way, your self-respect, regardless of the thoughts or behavior of others, comes from within. People can be sure of one thing at any given time: they won't be as good or bad as they say.

By exercising restraint to break these bad habits, you can simultaneously strengthen your self-controlled muscles and break bad habits that can undermine your career.

10 Bad Health Habits Are Not Good For You

It is not too late to regret your worst habits (smoking, drinking, overeating, etc.) and to live a happier and healthier life right away.

If You're Not Hungry, Snack:

Loss of normal contact with hunger and satiety can lead to overeating and unhealthy books, increasing the risk of diabetes, heart disease and other serious diseases. Moreover, when you eat junk food, your body will be filled with unhealthy ingredients. By paying close attention to signs of hunger and choosing healthy snacks, you can improve your diet, control your desires and avoid energy consumption. Your weight drops to a healthier level and replaces saturated fats with saturated and unsaturated fats, sugar, refined carbohydrates and nutritious foods.

Eat because you are hungry, not because you are suffering from stress, boredom, anger or sadness. If you feel a little full and not drunk, end up with food. Do not store unhealthy foods at home, or at least pay attention to healthy foods such as fruits, vegetables and nuts. Keep in mind that low-fat fats are sweet; whole grains are unhealthy carbohydrates. Also, if you are eating these healthy snacks, please eat them as follows: On the plate, sit at the table with a glass of water.

Spend a Lot of Time on the Couch in Front of the TV:

The more you watch TV, the fewer times you participate in physical exercise, the greater the likelihood of developing obesity and type 2 diabetes. By maintaining a healthy balance between TV and activity, you can burn more calories quickly, stay healthy and reduce the risk of health problems. Your health is better, your sleep is longer, your energy is more abundant, your mood is better, your mind is better, and you are more social.

Try limiting your TV to at least two hours a day and exercising for at least 30 minutes. Take advantage of both worlds by doing light exercises, such as walking or sitting while watching. Even some household tasks, such as vacuuming or washing clothes in advertising, can extend the calorie-burning period by up to 20 minutes. Avoid falling in front of the TV because it makes eating hundreds or thousands of calories very easy and hardly noticeable. This is another reason why watching TV shows is unhealthy.

Debt:

Worried that money can seriously harm your health. In a telephone study at Rutgers University, participants said financial pressures led to high blood pressure, depression, insomnia, headaches, digestive problems, pain, stomach ulcers, excessive drinking and weight gain. Keeping your money takes time can seriously affect yourself and your lifestyle, and be alert. In addition, it is very easy to restore the original habits. But for those successful, there are also many people, and the results are amazing. You can reduce stress and anxiety and better manage your life.

There are many ways to manage your money. Learn more about the principles and methods of personal finance, including credit cards, mortgages, budgets and investments. Create and manage budgets and track how much you invest each month and how much you spend. At least pay a monthly bill to start spending and prioritize credit cards at the highest interest rates. With automatic bill payment, you can be sure that you never have to deal with overdue fees. To ensure that part of your salary is automatically transferred to your savings account, you can make regular monthly transfers by managing your employer's or bank's online human resources. If you want to save more money, these habits are a good start for those who can save a lot of money.

Eat a Lot of Junk Food:

Two often eaten burgers and French fries, which are washed with excess soda or milk, can cause waist circumference and related health problems such as heart disease and diabetes. Unsaturated fats commonly found in fast foods increase triglycerides and LDL cholesterol, thereby increasing inflammation and promoting the formation of fat plates in the vascular wall. The health benefits of switching to a healthy diet are almost immediate and have long-term benefits.

First of all, it is not easy to change your lifestyle forever. Fast food is very convenient and affordable, and because of all the fat, salt and sugar, it is delicious. First, reduce it a little every week and reduce your purchase each time. For example, instead of soda water or salad instead of french fries. Don't lose or go to a fast-food restaurant, especially if you're not too hungry or don't eat. Cooking at home. You can save money by preparing healthy meals. For inconvenience, don't forget to enjoy a healthy meal at the supermarket or local sandwich shop. Read the best tips for a healthy diet used by dietitians.

Several Sunburns Every Summer:

If you want to sunbathe or try to maintain a golden tan, this will lead to ageing without knowing it. Sunbathing destroys elastic fibers, leaving skin soft and smooth and causing premature wrinkles, spots, freckles and discoloration. Most importantly, sunburn can cause skin cancer. If you book a trip to the tannery, it would be worse. Regardless of advertising tips, using a tanning layer will not produce a "safe" color. In fact, increases the risk of skin cancer and wrinkles.

Always use a high SPF sunscreen when in the sun. It can also help protect your skin by wearing a hat, sunglasses, long sleeves and trousers while holding onto shadows and during tanning. Arrange for a dermatologist to conduct an annual "check-up". Your doctor will examine your skin for abnormal changes. And keep your eyes on the skin. Improper substances should be examined by a doctor. If you can't live without a tan, you can do it yourself without cancer.

Always Make You Angry, Anxious, Or Nervous:

Unhealthy lifestyles produce a range of stress hormones that raise blood pressure and blood sugar, reduce body immunity, slow digestion and frustrate you. Natural stress should be a short-term response to threats, but modern life with chronic stress can have a profound impact on your health and obesity. Ingredients and excess weight in bad foods increase the risk of heart disease and diabetes.

How to solve this problem: It is useful to restore joy and control, and the health benefits will be enormous. The next time you feel stressed, try to control and relax. Yoga, meditation and deep breathing are good habits to reduce stress. Take advantage of your free time, relax in your hobbies, and indulge in this passion. Don't be afraid to accept your happiness, optimism and stupidity from time to time. Reducing stress can make you healthier, and a healthy lifestyle can lower stress levels and help you overcome stressful situations.

Breakfast When You Are Not Hungry:

The "rules" that you should not skip breakfast are incorrect. According to the New York Times, it relies on the wrong investigation of research and bias. Almost all studies at breakfast showed that this has nothing to do with it. Many self-reported studies have become victims of distortion and abuse inherent in casual language.

Solve the problem as follows: eat during hunger. If not, it is fast. Intermittent fasting - optional eating and drinking, fasting every day - has caused a lot of attention lately. Studies have shown that even if you do not eat food for a certain period of time, blood sugar still exists, which can stimulate metabolism and help the body become obese. Benefits include improved blood sugar control and one-day adjustment (better sleep); all of these can help prevent diabetes.

Drink Plenty of Alcohol:

If you drink a lot, alcohol can be poison. Women who ate two or more drinks daily and three or more men daily suffered significant liver damage and various risks of cancer, including liver and mouth cancer, hypertension and depression. Women who are more sensitive to alcohol than men develop heart disease, osteoporosis and even memory loss. Shortly after shortening or stopping, your digestive system will improve and you will sleep closely. Your blood sugar level drops and becomes more stable. Your blood pressure may drop in a healthier area, and even your mind will bounce back. Your liver and cardiovascular systems are healthier.

You don't have to kill Turkey. Adhere to the limits of health. Men drink two or fewer drinks a day, and women drink one cup a day. When you order a meal, you are more likely to drink slowly. Drink alcohol to avoid alcohol. If you can't stop, you'll realize you're addicted. Talk to your doctor and call a support group, such as AA. Ask your doctor if you need to check bone density, cancer and liver damage frequently. These 17 tips will help you reduce your alcohol intake, giving you a good start.

Smoking:

In health terms, there is no more harmful habit than smoking. Immediately caused 30% of heart disease deaths, 30% of cancer deaths and 80% to 90% of lung cancer deaths, plus an increased risk of oral, throat and bladder cancer. This bad habit also increases the risk of heart disease, stroke and high blood pressure in astronomy, as well as causing or aggravating respiratory diseases such as bronchitis and asthma attacks. After you stop taking it, the health benefits are almost instantaneous. Within a month, your lungs will improve and you will need to reduce your cough, become more active and have less difficulty breathing. Your taste, smell and strength have also improved.

Treat it as an addiction rather than a habit. Be prepared before you stop. Plan to stand in quiet weather - not on holiday or under pressure. If your first approach fails, develop a strategy to support the team and develop a plan B. Ask your doctor to stop smoking, such as bupropion, varenicline patches, nicotine or gum. Seek help or resources from friends and family, such as counselors, hotlines, and support groups. Finally, remember that failure is not a failure. Use these errors to identify and plan the personal barriers you want to block the next time you manage them. If you need additional help, check out 23 stop modes below.

Excessive Use of Painkillers and Sedatives:

If left untreated, prolonged use of prescribed painkillers can be addictive and cause more problems than they resolve. Even freely available medications such as ibuprofen or aspirin for arthritis or muscle pain can, over time, increase the risk of gastric ulcer, gastrointestinal bleeding, high blood pressure and heart attack. Signs that you're using too much of a sedative or sleeping pill include memory loss, excessive sleepiness, lack of response or confusion, and frequent falls. If you are comfortable with medication, you can continue to use it and make it a habit or addiction before you know it. With your commitment and support, you can give up the habit of taking soothing and prescribed painkillers. When the pills are stopped, your body can quickly recover from their effect.

Here's how to fix this: New pain relief strategies can relieve muscles, joints and headaches with fewer pills and side effects. Ask your doctor about chronic pain after switching to acetaminophen. It does not cause stomach irritation and does not raise blood pressure like aspirin and ibuprofen. Store ibuprofen in case of short-term acute pain recurrence. If you have a headache, consult your doctor. Migraines can often be stopped with the right medication. If you think you are addicted, ask a doctor who wants to treat you with prolonged pain, mood or sleeping pills. If you already trust them too much, ask for help if you can't stop. It is not bad to ask for help from family members, friends or your doctor. Read on to find out more about poor health habits. Doctors want to travel as soon as possible.

The Most Common Bad Habits in Young Children

Bad habits for young children can become serious problems in later life. In this sense, it is important that parents are aware of the warning signs and timely intervention to correct them. Children imitate the behavior of their peers. If children spend all their time on people with bad habits, they will accept it. This is very important when talking about correcting bad habits in young children.

When we repeat unconscious behavior, we usually form. Bad habits of young children can talk about physical or mental problems. Habits can lead to compulsive behavior and require the dissolution of a doctor or psychologist. Some bad habits for young children may directly affect your health. Others can influence relationships and family life. In both cases, it is important to correct bad habits quickly so that they are not permanent.

What Should I Know About Children's Bad Habits And Behaviors?

Parents believe that many of their children's habits and behaviors are distracting. If you want to change the unwanted behavior, it helps to understand why your child is doing it. Bad habits are often just an adaptation strategy. Your child can use this behavior when stressed, bored, frustrated, unhappy, insecure or tired. Many of these "bad" habits soothe and soothe the child.

In most cases, this behavior is just "phases" or habits - not serious medical problems - from which the child usually grows. However, managing behavior can be difficult. You should generally try to ignore bad habits. Shouting, habits and punishment are usually not enough to stop (and even amplify) the behavior. Praise, positive rewards (if your child does not) and patience are probably helpful.

Thumb and Finger Suck and Lollipop:

There are different types of nursing children who can spend their childhood and adolescence. Sucking thumbs and fingers usually starts in the first months of life. Many babies grow up well until their first birthday and stop most at the age of 5 under pressure from their peers. Lollipops and blankets are other common suction items.

Sucking has a calming and soothing effect and often helps children fall asleep. However, this can be problematic when permanent teeth come in (for example, at the age of 5) when the suction changes the shape of the child's teeth, palate or bite. If your child is using a pacifier, it is better to use the pacifier than to suck your thumb. Try to get rid of pacifier before the age of 4 years. Here are some ideas to get rid of the lollipop:

• Cut slits in the mouthpiece of the lollipop. This makes it less effective and children often lose interest.

• Let the pacifier come. Let your child put all her lollipops in a pot and spend the night on the lollipop fairy. Let "fairy" give a special treat to the big girl/boy who gives up his feed.

• If it is too hard for you to eat a cold turkey, ask your baby to place nappies in the bedroom each morning so it cannot be used for bedtime or lunch.

Hammer Your Head, Roll Your Head and Balance Your Body:

A blow to the head is when a child repeatedly beats his head against a solid object. Some children hit the head up to 80 times a day. This can be a burden for parents or guardians due to injuries. Often the child does not seem to suffer, but he is calm and satisfied. The habit usually starts at about 9 months of age and dissolves at about 2 months of age. Rolling of the head occurs when a baby rolls his head on his back. You can even scrub the hair completely from the back of the head.

Body swing occurs when a child swings, while sitting or sitting on his knees or elbows. This behavior usually starts at the age of 6 months and disappears at the age of 2 years. Most children play 15 minutes or less. As with head whipping, this often happens when you hear music or fall asleep. Hammering your head, rolling your head and cradling your body are common habits in your youth to comfort you. This behavior is often harmless but can be disturbing if your child also has developmental delays. Talk to your pediatrician about the habit that can help you decide if to worry.

Grinding Teeth:

Milling or milling usually affects more than half of normal children. Temporary teeth for more than 6 months are usually counted. 5 months after the arrival of permanent teeth. Grinding occurs primarily during sleep. Children usually grow up, but candidly continue to grow up. If adults have teeth in their jaws, this can be a problem because they can cause dental problems or TMJ disease. If your child bites an adult's teeth, you may need a dentist check.

Biting Or Rubbing Nails And Corneal Layers:

When the nail or the cornea repeatedly causes bleeding or injury to the nail layer, there is a problem with biting and picking up the nail. Like other habits, a positive empowerment strategy is the most effective way to stop behavior. When trying to catch a child, don't put your finger in your mouth or describe what his hand is doing. For example: "I found that you folded the paper with your fingers" or "Hold the ears with the cat's ears!" She likes it! ”

In addition, there are nail polish cakes that can help fools/cut nipples. Some families put administrative management first. You can put it on a bad gypsum vinegar.

Choose Nose:

Choosing the nose is one of the most unpleasant behaviors of parents and one of the most unacceptable behaviors in society. However, this is one of the most common habits of children and adults. Covering may cause infection, allergies or mild shock, which may cause nasal congestion. Forage will harden the nose and cause a vicious circle. The group is the most common cause of bleeding.

Tell your child that the listener's nose is not itchy, but use a paper towel to clean the nose and relieve itching. Explain that when he holds his nose, it spreads the bacteria to others. After picking up or discovering them, please continue to wash your hands. Vaseline can usually help the nose break several times a day and collect a vicious circle of irritating rhinitis. It is also helpful to keep your nose moist with some salt spray before going to bed. Talk to your child's doctor to relieve irritation to the nasal mucosa.

Stirring/Pulling:

Hair loss can be a sign of a medical problem, such as an infection or other illness. If your child has lost his hair, your child should see a doctor. However, curling or pulling light (resulting in minimal hair

71

loss) is another fact of self-confidence for babies and children. When a child relaxes or feels bored or tired, the thumb sucks more frequently. Children usually do not exceed habits alone.

It is a dense plucking, trichomoniasis form that can pull out the scalp, eyelashes, eyebrows and/or pubic hair. This rare disease usually suffers from possible psychological problems and requires a doctor to evaluate it.

Twitch:

Tic is a frequent cliché (contraction or movement). Exercise affects all parts of the body. The most common is facial expressions, especially blinking. Temporary tics usually begin in childhood or adolescence and last from one month to one year. On request, the child can automatically delete the hash tag within a few minutes to a few hours. Eavesdropping can sometimes be more frequent than at other times.

In rare cases, speech disorders or more complex problems represent acute Tourette syndrome. If the duration of convulsions is more than one year, or if the child is unable to remove them, it may indicate that the problem is more serious and should be checked by a pediatrician.

Unhealthy Diet:

Eating junk food today is a bad habit. Even some children just want to eat junk food. One of the consequences of this habit is childhood obesity and high blood pressure. To keep your child out of habit, prepare recipes that contain different foods and visually attract your child. If there are certain foods they do not like, replace them with other foods in the same food group. Allow your child to participate: he or she will eat something that will help them faster. The most common bad habits for young children

Eat Before TV:

Studies have shown that eating on TV leads to weight gain. The brains of children who focus on their favorite programs do not receive news when they are full, leading to overeating. In addition, meals prepared for the family should be an opportunity to sit down and talk about their day.

"Children imitate the behavior of their peers - if the child is with someone who has bad habits, they will accept him."

Rude and Offensive Language:

As mentioned earlier, children imitate what they see. When adults are rude to each other or speak a bad language at home, the child will develop a habit, which is difficult to correct. When children go out, they repeat the outrageous words of teachers and other adults. Corrections should start at home and give a better example.

Computers, Video Games and TV:

The technology and time you spend in front of the screen can range from casual to addicting. It even affects our health. Many children are reluctant to play outside because they are trapped in front of a computer or smartphone. Excessive time on the screen can also lead to sleep disorders and affect the social development of children. If you spend a lot of time playing or playing online, your child may be late for homework. To prevent or correct these bad habits in young children, set up routine procedures and make sure they do not stand in front of the screen for more than two hours in a row. However, technical searches can also hide potential problems. Many children with insecurity or fear rely on technology to escape. If you find any worse signs, please contact your doctor.

Place Your Thumb or Nose:

Sometimes, young children absorb their thumb instead of lollipops. This bad habit occurs early, but they usually disappear on their own. If not, please contact an expert to check if the child's captain has a problem. Choosing a nose is another uncomfortable exercise that can lead to nosebleeds. Young children usually do this without knowing it. Make sure your child knows what to do each time he puts his finger on his nose and that you break the habit.

Sleep Late:

Children need 11 to 13 hours of sleep a day. Night. If children cannot rest enough, they will feel disturbed, distracted, tired and indifferent. This can lead to amnesia and slow thinking. Insufficient sleep can cause hormonal imbalance. Developing good sleep habits and maintaining daily activities without exception are ways to change the habit. For example, allow your children to eat early and have them sleep by reading stories to develop new habits.

Poor Hygiene:

Hygiene is a prerequisite for good health and normal social life. Many babies don't want to bathe, or they don't always brush their teeth after eating. But this resistance can become a bad habit. Make sure the whole family wash their hands regularly, bathe every day, and brush their teeth regularly. Remember that children should restore their parents' habits and lead by example.

Masturbation:

Most children (boys and girls) play with their genitals regularly between the ages of 5 and 6. Masturbation is usually part of the child's normal development. It is important to remember that masturbation at this age is not sexual for children. If you are worried about your child's masturbation, a pediatrician may be a useful resource.

Chapter 4

How to Make Good Habits?

How To Develop Good Habits: Tips To Research

Have you ever wondered why some people seem so busy? When they say "I'm going to ...", they start to exercise, eat, organize, read more and so on. They know they will. However, if you try to pursue similar goals, this is another matter. You may be with them for a while, but eventually, you will lose motivation and surrender.

If this happens often, it is easy to feel depressed and frustrated. However, it is not difficult and painful to develop and maintain good habits. It's very easy. So have fun. Most of us are humans, animals, so it must be easy to develop good habits - well! Not always

The problem is that we are satisfied with doing the same thing every day. We often stick to daily plans, regardless of consistency or efficiency. Why the change?

Unfortunately, all our habits are unhealthy or not good. If we used to go home after work every day and drink some alcohol to relax, instead of going to the mill to blow up steam, it would endanger our health. Or if we tend to watch TV and drink lemonade at night instead of eating vegetables and juice, it will have bad health consequences. If we put smoking, reduce stress/anxiety, overeat or frustrate others, we must recognize that these habits must be changed or eliminated.

How to develop good living habits:

Start Small:

Most people want to make big changes as soon as possible. Every week, they move from zero hours to four hours, they switch to a healthy diet at night, meditate for 20 minutes a day, and in the past, they spent only five minutes. The problem, of course, is that it requires a lot of willpower. Studies have shown that widows work like muscles. If you use it a lot, it will be very tiring. If so, it is likely to stop. A woman exercises pressure-raising exercises and the dog develops good habits on her back. The solution to this problem is to start small and do not need to:

• Start with five pumps instead of 50 per day.

• No need to change your eating habits, add vegetables every lunch.

• You don't have to spend 20 minutes on recovery every day but start in two minutes.

• Always focus on identifying true habits. Please do not increase your workload until your daily work is normal.

Dye Your Habits:

Have you ever noticed how difficult it is to leave a project if you put a lot of effort into it?

We can capitalize on this trend through the comedy actor Jerry Seinfeld's "Don't Break the Chain" strategy.

Seinfeld used this method to make it better comic by writing a new joke every day. Every time you finish typing on that day, he puts a big red X in the day's calendar. Within a few days, he had a series he didn't want to break.

This is a very smart strategy that allows you to visually remember what you spend on your habits. You may find that the longer the chain, the more difficult it is to maintain the chain.

Buy a calendar and check the calendar to get used to your habits. Your only task is not to break slavery.

Have a Clear Intention:

If you take your new habits seriously, these mysterious intentions such as "I have to go to the gym three times this week" will not help. Studies have shown that you will know a lot when accurately determining when and where behavior occurs.

Here are three effective strategies to do this:

Create an Execution Target. Update your habits to "if / then". Example: "When I finish breakfast, I'll make five pumps."

Use of General Stacking. Combine your new habits and past behavior by entering the following statement: "Before / before [established habits], you became [new habits]." For example: "Once I leave the office, I will take some steps."

Complete plan. This seems obvious, but few people actually use it. The plan will be completed. If your habits are really important to you, please think about them on your agenda. As with a large business meeting, leave room for it in the plan.

Celebrate Your Lean Profit:

If you are like most people, it's better to reward yourself than to be good. When it comes to controlling ourselves for any reason, we seem to prefer a whip of carrots. It's unfortunate because research shows that celebrating your progress is important to you. When you reward yourself for progress, no matter how small, you will activate the rewards circle in your mind. This will release important chemicals that make you feel full and proud. In turn, these feelings can make you act and be more successful in the future. No matter how fast the pace, you should take your first step in the right direction.

Environmental Design:

Your environment determines your behavior in several ways. Have you ever gone to the kitchen and saw a plate of cookies on the table just because they ate in front of you? In this case, you know what I mean. Mihaly Csikszentmihalyi, a professor of psychology and best-selling author, provides an excellent framework for designing your environment to support the habits you need. His advice is to deliberately change the "activation energy" in your habits. The idea is that all of your habits require a certain amount of energy to achieve. Moreover, the more activation power you need, the less chance you will get involved. Suppose you want to read more books, but usually, watch TV. What you need to do is:

• Reduce the activation energy you need (read books). For example, place a good book next to the sofa in the living room.

• Increase activation energy from your bad habits (TV). For example, place the TV set remotely in another room.

• By changing the energizing behavior of the behavior, you can move in the right direction.

Be With Followers:

The people around us have a surprisingly large impact on our behavior. A study shows that even if your friends live hundreds of miles away, the risk of obesity in obese friends is 57%! Other studies have shown that we tend to think about the same goals and pursue them in the same way most people spend most of their time. One way to dramatically increase your chances of success is to make sure you have the right people in your area.

Three elderly people go hand in hand and develop good habits

• If you want to develop a healthy habit, but all your friends are not healthy, it is time to meet new people.

• If you want to do wonderful things in your life, but are surrounded by pessimists who demean you, it's time to create a support group to motivate and support you in case of failure.

• They represent the average of the five people you spend most of the time with. Let it be.

Develop Habits In Advance:

Imagine that 5:18 pm and the alarm sounds. If your brain starts to be rational, the plan to go to the gym before the exercise will be threatened within seconds.

"Well, I'm really tired. I want to know if I'm too tired to go to the gym after work or work out in the gym tomorrow morning. Yes, press the sleep button."

But then you still remember the friends you promised, at the gym 7. Or you can follow the training program and send a friend $ 50 to work each time you leave the gym. You can also tell your family, blog readers, and Facebook friends publicly that you need to follow a 30-day training program. Going back to sleep is not an attractive option. If you sign up this way, you can add a responsible layer that can be used to confirm even if you are having difficulties.

When developing new habits, you must introduce the mentality of scientists and professionals. Think about everything you do in a behavioral experiment, and each setback will provide valuable data for your next step.

Determine the Habit:

As mentioned earlier, we usually ignore our good and bad habits. Therefore, we must be the first to realize this. If this cough becomes worse, or if we take a few steps after climbing, it may be because of smoking (smoking, lack of exercise) or lack of good habits (exercise). Our money may be wasted, which means that we have a bad habit of spending too much, or not a good habit of exercising, respecting and respecting the budget. It's time to explore our habits!

Make a Decision and Then Commit to Change:

Of course, this is easier said than done. How many times have we said: "Yes, I have to exercise more food and eat better, don't worry, I'll be there sooner or later."

Unfortunately, bad habits are hard to change. The more you stop working, especially with regard to health, the healthier you or your health will be. A conscious commitment is required to operate the wheels.

Discover Your Triggers and Obstacles:

If you don't know the operator or you're not ready for the inevitable obstacles, get ready for failure. To develop good habits, we need to pay attention to our habits. At a time of weakness and weakness, we all need frustrating support or rescue. Do not use alcohol, drugs and excessive drug use.

If you have an unpleasant event at work or on your way home, look for a healthy alternative to routine exercise. Each of us has a bad day, but we don't need to develop bad habits to relieve stress. Similarly, boredom, anger or fear should not lead to bad habits. Look for healthy ways to solve triggers and obstacles.

Plan Virtues in Life:

Benjamin Franklin has a good plan to overcome his bad habits and replace them with good ones. He developed a process that listed 13 virtues that he considered important and then conducted research. He focuses on virtue every week and forgets good habits for 13 weeks. Every weekend, he felt he mastered the bad habit and continued until next week.

In this process, he recorded his success with virtue. Because some virtues help others win, he orders them to start calming down in a certain order, because "this tends to keep the head alert and keep his head fresh and transparent."

It's very effective for people trying to develop new good habits - you should actually be vigilant to make sure you respect them! After kindness, he worked quietly, because knowledge was obtained with the best ear of the language.

Franklin has rhymes, cause and purpose of every virtue. He believes that developing good habits is free to maintain the order he really wants to achieve in life. Once he develops normally, his design will help him focus on achieving all the other virtues. For entertainment, here's a list of Benjamin Franklin's virtues. You can create similar lists to include good habits in your lifestyle.

List of virtues included in the life of Benjamin Franklin:

Moderation - do not eat boredom; do not drink too much.

Silence - do not talk, but what can benefit others or yourself? Avoid trivial conversations.

Demand - Allow all your property to have a location of your own; allow each part of your business to have its own time

Decide - Decide to do what you want to do. Do it according to your solution.

Finance - Don't do anything to help others or yourself. Don't waste anything.

Industry - don't waste time; always busy with some useful things; remove all unnecessary processes.

Integrity - do not use abusive fraud; think in good faith, if you speak, please speak accordingly.

Justice - If you do not harm or ignore the benefits you have, this is incorrect.

Moderate - avoid extremism; forget as much as possible with annoying wounds.

Clean - does not tolerate impurities in your body, clothes or apartment.

Comfort - Do not interfere with minor, repetitive or inevitable accidents.

Chastity - Do not use the game too often, but for health or future generations, never use the game for boring, weakness or infringement on your safety or other reputation.

Apply Visualization and Validation:

Visualization and validation is a great way to incorporate new habits into your daily work. While visualization is a powerful tool to motivate motivation and energy, it is certain to program the subconscious mind with the correct attitude to develop new habits. Together, they make you feel good about behavior and imagine what leads to new habits. When using visualization and verification, it is certainly easy to develop good habits.

Ask for Help from your Family and Friends:

Tell people what you want to achieve. This way, they will know whether you pass through the desert or walk instead of stopping at the bar while you return. When your friends know you are serious about developing a habit of good habits, it not only helps you get rid of temptation but also encourages you and supports you morally. We all need support to achieve our goals!

Find Healthy Ways to Reward Yourself:

One reason why we develop so many bad habits is that we feel good even if it is temporary. Good experiences calm or subside when we feel stressed, depressed or out of control. For example, you can eat too much and feel good, but it feels bad. The same applies to heavy smoking or drinking. When you are in the wild, you will feel comfortable and worry-free, but then you will regret it and promise to stop as soon as possible.

So if you work well, you can prevent yourself from falling and returning to old bad habits, please reward yourself. Give yourself a new book, film, concert, or exercise. If you have money, please visit a friend you haven't seen in a long time and visit the art gallery or bar in the city center.

The biggest benefit to developing good habits is that when they reappear, they adapt quickly. Everything you do in a suitable environment for a long time will eventually become a habit, and if so, you won't have to work hard. It is good to develop good habits!

Now You Can Do Three Simple Things to Create Better Habits

It may be difficult to develop good habits. This is especially true if you want to keep it for a long time. Fortunately, there are simple strategies to help you develop good habits and eliminate bad habits.

I'm not saying that these ideas are the only way to develop good habits - there are many - but these simple steps can help you achieve most of your health and practical goals. And your life. In this sense, you can now do three things to develop good habits.

Start Usually Very Simple, You Cannot Say No:

The most important thing when developing a new habit is to be consistent. The way you run today doesn't matter. Sustainable efforts are different. That's why it's so easy to develop a new habit that you can't help tell. In fact, starting a new behavior should be so easy that it is almost absurd.

• Want to develop exercise habits? Your goal is to train for one minute today.

• Do you want to develop your writing habits? Your goal is to write three sentences today.

• Do you want to develop good eating habits? Their goal is to get a healthy diet this week.

It doesn't matter if you start small because you have time to understand its intensity later. You don't have to go to Cross Fit immediately, write a book, or change your eating habits.

It's easy to compare what others are doing or feel the need to improve performance and do more. Don't let these feelings stop you.

Prove that you can keep small things for 30 days. If you are told and remain the same, you may be concerned about the increased difficulty.

At first, implementation is not important. In the long run, it doesn't matter if you insist on one or two good things. Make new habits that simple, you cannot refuse.

Take Some Time to Understand The Factors That Prevent You From Moving Forward Accurately:

I recently spoke to a reader named Jane. She will exercise regularly, but she always thinks she is "the type that doesn't like training."

Jane decided to abandon the habit and found that she didn't really practice it, which disturbed her. Instead, she doesn't like going to the gym, going somewhere for 20 minutes and then exercising. They also don't like going to public places to work for others. These are real obstacles to his usual practice.

When she realized this, Jane wanted to know how to simplify training. I bought a yoga video and started training at home two nights a week. She is also a teacher, and her school offers classes. I started taking this course because it meant that she didn't have to go anywhere else or spend a lot of time preparing for training.

Jane insisted on a few months of training programs. "Maybe you can't solve everything you don't like, but finding a way to overcome one or two of these obstacles may be that you're keen to ... achieve and achieve your goals," she said.

People who follow good habits will know exactly why their progress is impeded.

You might think of yourself as "the type of people who don't like training," "the types of people who don't organize," or "the types of people who like candy." However, in most cases, you are not destined to fail in these areas. Don't make a general statement about your habits, but break them down into smaller parts and identify areas that make you inconsistent.

Once you know what specific process elements are preventing you from moving forward, you can develop a solution to resolve this issue.

Develop A Plan:

Often, folk and strength trainer Dan John tells his athletes: "You're not good enough and disappointing." If you want to develop new habits, the same is true. Did you expect success from the beginning? Perfect, even people who have done it for many years often make mistakes?

You should learn not to judge yourself, and if you make a mistake, you will not feel it. Instead, you should focus on making plans to get back on track as quickly as possible.

The following three strategies can help you...

• Set the table instead of the due date.

• Forget about performance and focus on building new identities.

• Make it your new motto: "Don't miss it twice."

I think the "don't miss" mentality is particularly useful. I may miss the course, but I won't miss it twice in a row. Maybe I'll eat the entire pizza and then eat a healthy meal. Maybe I forgot to meditate today, but I'm leaving with Zain tomorrow morning.

If you give up your habits, you won't get it wrong. This makes you natural. The reason why service providers are different in that they are quickly backed on track. Make sure you have a plan just in case.

Unexpected Ways To Develop Good Habits - And Maintain Good Habits

Sometimes you need to adjust your habits. How is it?

The fastest way to achieve your dreams is to participate. Once you're busy, nothing will bother you unless you have bad habits. However, if the bet is strong enough, it will break these habits.

Nothing is more effective than good habits. We all know that high performing people have good habits. But how can we develop and maintain it?

Your custom is yours. Your inner peace and happiness usually come from your habits.

You decide about your habits. Success and joy come when you focus on what you control. When you focus on situations or people you can't control, you lose control and enter into a state of frustration and despair.

Good habits develop a positive attitude. By focusing on behaviors that you can control, you can plan and take action. Hope to solve the problem is usually enough to change the mood and thus change the result.

Develop and maintain good habits about the outcome process.

Yes, we definitely want the results. In the end, the results are important. However, for best results, do not focus on the ultimate goal, but focus on what you need to achieve and control those steps.

The following are some processes to ensure good implementation practices:

Cultivate Clarity:

Brendon Borchard is a great coach recognized by Oprah and knows:

"You have to know who you are, what you value, what your strengths and weaknesses are, where you go, and with that knowledge, you will feel comfortable about yourself and your life."

In other words, know and decide what you want. Know who you are and what you want to know.

If you have clear intentions and specific goals, you will become the "reason" to be the most important motivation for you. For this purpose, there is no work or sacrifice too much.

Achieve your weekly goals. Check your campaigns daily.

Focus on Your Daily Work:

You may be able to perform these tasks using autopilot. Make your habits part of your daily work. Write it down from the list.

If you want a better customer, check what you need to do to attract them and then develop the habits associated with a particular offer. Enter it into your schedule.

Every goal is possible. Lie down and write on it. "The key to victory is to make a good routine," said Charles Duhig's best-selling author.

Reward Desired Behavior:

Bad habits will be rewarded, otherwise, there will be no bad habits.

"Good habits are as addictive as bad habits, and they are more valuable," says Harvey Mackey, a successful sales executive. Of course, it's easier said than done, but you can.

Don't change the bonus - just change the method used. Find the benefits that interest you and use them to match good behavior with desired results.

Record your Progress:

Celebrate the victory. Consider the error. Develop plans to widen the profit gap and strategies to reduce errors.

As the late Jim Ron said, "A life worth living is a life worth tolerating."

Habits are illogical without proper thinking. By applying your personal feelings, you can accelerate your progress.

Find your Super Supporter:

You need to spend time with someone who can help you develop your habits. Don't take me away and bring him to Oprah Winfrey, who once said: "Only with people who want to take you to a higher position.

Find the most active people you know and ask them to be accountable to you.

They want to make sure you are on the right track and do it with a positive attitude. This type of support is needed to know that you agree with your values and that your behavior corresponds to "why."

Habits can help you do things consistently without having to think about the process. Habits will succeed or fail. The advantage is that habits can change.

The choice you choose today is usually tomorrow. If you think you have the ability to adapt and change, you can develop a habit that increases your potential.

Chapter 5

Understand What Triggers your Bad Habits?

As some people hate to admit it, people are not perfect. We know what we need to do - like sports, eating well and getting plenty of sleep - but not having to keep up. And sometimes what happens when there is a mistake, a rush or control over bad behavior. The good news is that it can leave you feeling bad and we are here to help you with this.

Let's face it; we all have bad habits. We can bite our nails or break our ankles. Some of us often interact with people or wait for others. All these bad habits are hard to break. But fear not!

Identify the behavior you want to change

The idea that you have a "bad attitude" is not enough: you need to be clear on which behavior you want to change. On one occasion, a community relations specialist said, "You have to push a behavior that is broken by thinking about certain behaviors, such as not putting shoes in the living room. But put it in your closet. Don't eat in front of the TV, but at the table; Run for half an hour five days a week; Send your friends' white paper once a day instead of sending it in vain or in bad shape.

You need to know exactly how you are going to work.

Understand what triggers your bad habits

Understanding how we make decisions is the key to overcoming all kinds of bad habits, including those related to money. We often repeat bad habits without noticing that we are doing them. However, five clues usually contribute to any bad habit. If we are aware of them, we can learn what is behind these behaviors.

• Location

• Times

• Emotional state

• Other people

• An immediate preceding action

Write down these five things each time you have the same bad habit. If you notice similarities, learn what the triggers habit and you can take the necessary steps to resolve them.

Go slow and make small changes

Making better new habits requires time and effort, but breaking good bad habits can be even more difficult. So be patient with yourself and instead of making drastic adjustments, focusing on one habit and the smallest steps you can take to "trick your inner caveman" cream in your coffee to low-fat milk can make a big difference, in the long run, make and. encourage additional small but meaningful changes.

Spend month thinking about your habit before taking action

You may now be itching to correct this behavior, but as mentioned above, it may take some time. Before trying to change a habit, you should first think for a month, list all the reasons you want to stop each time you catch it, and so on. You can be better prepared to overcome this plan.

Remember your future self to avoid bad behavior

Even with the best of intentions, we fall into bad habits when our power is diminished. For example, you can promise to drink only two glasses of wine when you go out to make friends, but forget this promise as soon as you enter the food line. Try to set reminders for the weakest moments in your calendar.

Teach yourself to think differently about your negative

Even if we hate the behaviors we do, such as smoking or biting our nails, we love to continue because they give us something exciting or rewarding. Remember to think of all the positive thoughts or feelings about your bad habits, and change them to remind you of the negative ones. In other words, in this case, it is good to feel like a hater.

Change Your Habit Loop

Recently, over the past two decades, scientists have discovered that habits are stored differently in the brain and traditional memories. In short, the habit consists of a clue, a routine, and an endpoint.

Usually, an emotion triggers a behavior that ends when that emotional need is satisfied. There are two effects of these results:

First, your habits are hard-coded in your brain. This means that they cannot be removed. Once educated, they stay with you forever. This is why alcoholics or drug addicts are dependent on their addiction, sometimes even after decades of "clean" life. An old trigger triggered an old behavior.

Secondly, there is no way to get rid of the old habit. You can only remove it by lobotomy. However, you can replace it with a new routine. The most effective (and most cruel) method is to reprogram the behavior.

For example, when you take alcohol, when you are afraid of the future, you use the same feeling (anxiety) to adopt a new behavior (for example, prayer).

Why is it cruel? Well, to make a new behavior a habit, you have to make it stronger than the old habit. There are other factors, such as your attention to the new behavior, but in general, it depends on the number of repetitions. So if you drank twice a week for a decade, you had to pray three times a week for about seven years. The good news is that you will never return to the old routine when the new behavior solidifies. Another thing is that you need to zoom in and identify with surgical precision exactly what triggers, routines and endpoints are.

When is it the best?

This method is very universal. This is the most effective method for adopting "physical" habits: nail bite, facial expressions, "involuntary" gestures or even unwanted language patterns.

However, it can be used to replace bad habits with new ones.

Track to Reinforce Your Determination

It's not a way to break a bad habit, but it's still useful for getting rid of a habit. In the case of the small step approach, this is pretty obvious. If you want to limit yourself to a few cigarettes, you have to follow their numbers, right?

It's also a good idea to keep track of what works and what does not work when dealing with your usual loop. Monitoring is about making sure you're not used to your bad habits that day. However, you can use tracking even when you leave the cold turkey, which shows the biggest advantage of this tool. When you give up your bad habit, start counting the days without your addiction. And you build a series that motivates you to continue.

If you are pure for a day and not even a year has passed, it's a bliss. The second day of the chain is an event to celebrate. Then comes the first week, the first month, 100 consecutive days, the first year. These milestones will give you a sense of accomplishment even if you have done nothing. That was the goal of the exercise, was not it? Also, monitoring works the same way to create good habits. It focuses your attention on what is important and motivates you to continue.

It also offers invaluable data points that help you identify dangerous points and pitfalls. At first, it helps to identify your triggers. Later, it is useful to check whether you have implemented a new routine successfully or how often you avoid or modify the triggers of your negative behavior.

When is it best?

It's best to track your habits every single time. Whether you break the bad habit or build a positive one, you should pay close attention to your progress.

Focus on Good Habits

This method kills your bad habits with hunger. You see, getting rid of a bad habit draws your attention to the negative aspects of your life. He feels more restrictive than liberating. They watch each other all the time and refuse the "joys".

Yes, you know that in the long run, it's best to avoid cigarettes, vodka, drugs, masturbation, sweets, and nail-biting until your fingers look like bloody pulp, eat or explode of rage. But these bad behaviors are part of you. These are the backup mechanisms that have helped you cope with stress, anxiety or low self-esteem. Without them, your life seems even less bearable.

Rather than focusing on what you cannot do anymore, focus on new activities that have a positive impact on your life. You devote all your energy to improving your life, rather than avoiding what is wrong.

Quit Cold Turkey

You just stop giving in to your habit, not even from a day, but from now on. You say to yourself: "Stop!" "Not anymore!" Or "It ends now!"

This is the theory. It's not so easy to get rid of a habit. It is anchored in your brain. When its trigger repeats, the old behavior ignites. This is the biggest weakness of this method.

If an old pattern comes up and you only slip once, it's often a big problem. You feel as if you are wasting abstinence all the time. You are so depressed by self-deception that when an old habit is back, you are completely lost in your old habits. But there is also strength in such an approach. If you leave the cold turkey and keep your determination for a few days, show yourself that you can change.

Tips for improving this approach:

Make it your identity

Identify yourself to break your bad habit; I say to you: I am a human who does not ... [insert your destructible behavior]. Self-expression can be a weak strategy, especially if you have a lying claim. If you post several times a day in the mail for years and you say "I'm not angry," it might sound like a fairy tale.

In that case, modify the statement:

• "I want to be a person who doesn't get angry."

• "I'm becoming a person who doesn't get angry."

"Just today"

Tell yourself that you abstain from your bad behavior just for today. The prospect of giving up a bad habit, which has been part of your life for years or decades, can be overwhelming. You have so long succumbed to this behavior that you do not want to break it anymore.

But you can imagine abstinence for a day. The next day, you focus on your survival only that day. And so on. In a few days, you will start building a series, and then add some extra motivation to make the transition easier.

The ritual of destruction

You apply and confirm your decision by a dramatic act (or simply significant). If you stop drinking alcohol, you can break all the bottles in your house. If you stop lying, you can confess something terrible to your friend. If you stop watching TV, you can destroy your TV.

When is it the best?

Surprisingly, this method works well for dependencies.

If you feel a slave to harmful behavior, if you know that it is destructive to you, your loved ones and your future, it is easier to develop a strong motivation. It gives you the right impetus, "Stop!" "No more!" Or "It ends now!"

Adjusting Your Mindset

Take complete responsibility for your actions

You are the king or queen of your actions - no one is responsible like you. If you stay behind the driver's seat after three excessive drinks, it's up to you. In a way, this may be more convenient than taking a bus or calling a cab, but this remains your choice. Whether you like it or not, at some point you decide for yourself.

If you realize that you are fully responsible for your actions, you may feel overwhelmed or even paralyzed at first. You begin to realize that each of your actions has an impact and that these effects are very different from those you originally envisaged. It's a scary thought.

In the end, however, it is important to take responsibility for your actions. You are the creator of your destiny. In some standards, no one else can tell you what to do. Taking full responsibility for your actions gives you freedom. You begin to understand how habits can be metaphorical chains and how they can free you when they are broken.

Start scrutinizing the consequences and rewards of your habits

Create a simple pros/cons list of your habits. Try to treat yourself viciously and relentlessly. You can do it here is a list pro/contra e.g. smoking:

Pros:

• The feeling of calm and energy thanks to nicotine

• help with short-term stress

• Opportunity for social icebreakers

• helps me feel elegant

Cons:

• Many and harmful long-term health problems

• Addictive very quickly

• Expensive

• Violence reduces my life by several years

Start balancing short-term benefits with long-term consequences

Usually, we justify the practice of a habit we know bad because we place a disproportionate value on short-term benefits over long-term effects. And that's because we do not see the long-term effects - they are distant, difficult to judge, sometimes uncertain. It is much easier to see and feel the benefits in the short term.

For example, you may be a breakfast captain. They try to lose weight and convince themselves to do so. In the short term, you can lose a few pounds and feel better in your body. But in the long run, those pounds will probably come back (because you are not dieting properly) and you are planting the seeds of an eating disorder.

Psychological Concepts That Make You Better at Breaking Bad Habits

Most of the things you do every day are based on your habits: the way you get ready in the morning, the round trip to the office, and the same food that you always bring on the way home.

It's not necessarily a bad thing. Habits give a structure of life. They provide stability. They help you focus on the important things. Entering the autopilot is part of what makes the world move. Only when you start doing self-destructing things in this autopilot mode does a habit become something you can break. This is a difficult task for which there is a neurological reason. The researchers found that neural patterns are formed around repeated behavior. The more you do these things, the more these neuronal connections become strong.

If you're struggling to break a bad habit, try changing the cabling of your brain. But your brain is designed to love habits that require far less mental energy than critical thinking or conscious decisions and therefore defends itself against the prospect of change. The good news is that you can gain an advantage by understanding the psychological concepts that underlie normal education.

Cognitive dissonance

Most people know that their bad habits are bad for them, but this knowledge is not usually enough to prevent someone from smoking another cigarette or delaying this tedious job on the eve of the set deadline. It is cognitive dissonance, the psychological expression of persistent behavior that contradicts your beliefs.

An investigation revealed that, contrary to a widespread belief, it is not ignorance that maintains bad habits. "We assume it's ignorant and that the way to fix yourself is to tell you how bad this habit is or how good your life will be without it." But if ignorance was the real driving force, people would give up their habit if they were better informed.

In most cases, however, they neutralize this knowledge by emphasizing the benefits of habit (reducing stress through smoking, gaining leisure time by delaying) or a negative effect associated with stopping smoking. The frustration of having to ignore plans to tackle something on your to-do list). Knowing that something is unhealthy, but invoking reasons to do so is still a classic cognitive dissonance.

To train your brain out of this pattern, you need to find a way to bring your behavior into conformity with your beliefs. One tactic that can help is a cost-benefit analysis in which you continue your habit and use facts to overcome the wrong arguments that compel you to stick to it. Do not hesitate: yes, it would be more fun to go to dinner tonight and postpone the emails you wanted to send, and you hate it when you feel yourself being banned from your projects. On the other hand, you've already done it and it almost always means forgetting some of them and missing appointments.

Automaticity

All the habits exist in a spectrum of automatisms, the capacity of the brain to adopt complete behaviors without you thinking about it. Because of this, you can talk while driving at the same time.

For each person in each context, you can insert a common behavior in that spectrum. When you calculate and make decisions, it's not a habit. If you do something that you have done millions of times, you are in the autopilot. The outermost point of the spectrum is a reflex.

When behavior becomes a habit, it is almost always triggered by something. Trigger detection is the first step to avoid the resulting behavior. For example, if you place your plate in the sink to put a bowl of ice in the freezer, you can voluntarily replace it with a glass of ice water.

Automation is your goal when it comes to creating new and better habits, and it will be built gradually.

To put this into practice, first select a trigger. For example, if you want to get into the habit of flossing regularly, tell yourself that you have only one tooth left after brushing. The key is to start with something that seems feasible. Even if you do not want to, a tooth only takes a second. After all, you will usually clean your mouth without having to force yourself.

It's important to think strategically about your trigger if you want the behavior to last. For example, "I pump after peeing." Most people go to the bathroom at least several times a day, and some pumps after peeing only take a few seconds to turn them off.

"If you succeed, something can be part of your life immediately, if you cannot take out the trash, it's not a problem of will, it's a design problem, do not prepare, re-design -the."

Emotional regulation

Much of the usual education is emotionally related - in particular, people are conditioned to react to emotions with certain behaviors. When your phone rings in your pocket, your immediate emotional response is interest. Without thinking, you take it out to see the text message. A stressful situation can cause you to pay for something. Routine problems can cause you to accidentally burst.

Emotional reactions are hard to change, but they can be done. Adjusting your emotions is like forming other habits: start by focusing on the desired outcome, and then choose a behavior that will help you achieve it.

"In the morning, when you wake up and put your feet on the floor, you say, 'It will be a beautiful day.' It is a habit designed to counteract what most of us are conditioned to feel when we get up for the first time: bored on awakening and worried about the task list of the day. Regulating your emotions to tend to happiness and optimism from the first moments of the day can cause ripples. The trajectory of your day and distort your perception of everything that happens more positively.

You can also use your existing feelings about certain behaviors to create a healthier routine. People tend to believe that creating healthy and positive habits is a buzzword because you have to commit to doing things that you do not want to do much. But that does not have to be so. You will build better and faster your habits if you have fun.

"If you hate the treadmill but want to get used to training, will you have to stay on the treadmill for an hour?" No, be sure to choose the habits and behaviors that you like and want in your life.

Tell Others About Your Goals

When we talk about one goal to others and we do not do it, we are "punished" by shame and the feeling of leaving other people an embarrassment. Although shame is not necessarily the ideal motivator, it can be very effective.

When you talk to others about your goals, preferably those who support them, you are more likely to respect them because you do not have to tell your friends that you have failed. Say only to friends who do not lead you to your bad habit or make fun of your relapse. They want support, not ridicule!

To break a bad habit and replace it with a good one

Bad habits interrupt your life and prevent you from achieving your goals. They endanger your health - mentally and physically. And they waste your time and energy.

Why are we doing it again? And above all, can you do something about it?

What causes bad habits?

Most of your bad habits are caused by two things...

Stress and boredom

Bad habits are usually just a way to deal with stress and boredom. Anything can be an easy response to stress and boredom, whether it's nagging, excessive use during shopping, drinking on weekends or wasting time on the Internet. But that does not have to be like that. You can learn new, healthy ways to deal with stress and boredom, which you can then use instead of your bad habits.

Of course, sometimes the stress or boredom on the surface is caused by deeper problems. It can be hard to think about these problems, but if you want to make changes, you must be honest with yourself. Are there any beliefs or reasons behind bad habits? Is there anything deeper - a fear, an event or a limiting belief - that makes you cling to something bad for you?

Recognizing the causes of your bad habits is crucial to overcoming them.

You don't eliminate a bad habit, you replace it

Any habits you have - good or bad - are for a reason in your life. In a sense, these behaviors bring you an advantage, even if they are otherwise bad for you.

Sometimes the benefits are biological, as is the case with smoking or drugs. Sometimes it's emotional, like staying in a relationship that's bad for you. In many cases, your bad habit is an easy way to deal with stress. For example, biting your nails, pulling your hair, kicking your feet, clenching your jaw, etc. These "benefits" or reasons also apply to bad habits.

For example, if you open your inbox when you turn on your computer, you may feel connected. At the same time, watching all these emails destroys your productivity, divides your attention and overwhelms you with stress. But it prevents you from feeling "missed" ... and you do it again. Because bad habits have an advantage in your life, it is very difficult to eliminate them easily. Instead, you must replace a bad habit with a new habit that offers similar benefits.

For example, if you smoke while stressed, it is a bad plan to quit smoking when this happens. Instead, you should find another way to deal with stress, and insert this new behavior instead of smoking.

In other words, bad habits fulfill certain needs of your life. And for that reason, it is better to replace your bad habits with healthier behaviors that meet the same need. If you expect to simply eliminate bad habits without replacing them, then you will have some needs that are not met and it will be difficult to stick to a routine for a very long time that says you do not should do.

Have a better reason to quit

Even if you replace a "bad" habit with a better one, the original vice sometimes has a stronger biological "reward" than its replacement. For example, your brain knows that chewing gum is not nicotine and does not produce the same euphoric feeling as smoking a cigarette, he says. This is where the importance of intrinsic motivation comes into play.

Intellectually, we know that stopping is good for your health, and limiting the number of burgers we eat can help us lose weight. But changing habits for certain personal reasons (quitting smoking can mean spending more years with your family or eating healthier, and giving you more energy for the outdoor adventures you love), offers a dose from increased motivation.

Chapter 6

How to Get Rid of Bad Habits?

Everyone has bad habits. Now some people are less than others and the habits of some people are heavier than others, but we all have them.

The big thing is we don't have to. We can all make some changes.

There are two types of negative behaviors: those you know you have, while others may not see them, and others you may not know you have, but others are well aware of them.

How can you get rid of bad habits if you don't know you have it? The answer is simple but difficult: Ask someone, to be honest with you. You may be afraid of embarrassment, but do you want everyone to speak behind your back? Be courageous and ask. Ask the one who loves you and enjoy it. Be compassionate and not defend yourself. Just accept it and work on it.

What about those we know? These are difficult. Why not? You have to be tough if you know them and still have them. If they are not tough, they will be in bad shape in the past.

Most people have behaviors in their life that they need or want to change. Just because they are put in one direction does not mean it will remain forever. The key to changing people's relationships to exercise, productivity, eating, thinking, and even personality is to understand their behavior and change their relationships.

There are several articles on the Internet that provide information on criminal behavior. The first step is to acknowledge the wrong practices and promise to change. A real need to be there! Then develop a work plan to alleviate the transmission problem. Staying away from the routine is often the best time to get rid of bad habits. Holidays are the perfect example, where your daily life changes completely and so does your content.

The road to success is not easy and mistakes are failures. In this situation, evaluate why you are back on the model to better understand your weaknesses and remember your problem points. Then back to your plan to make the breakup a success. If necessary, take the blame for the failure and make it possible for you to teach it to others to avoid the punishment.

When done poorly, it can help to develop new behaviors. For example, if you quit smoking, you could use up the stairs every time you feel the urge to smoke. Be sure to reward yourself for your accomplishments to incorporate new habits. Save the money you cannot spend and you will have enough money for advanced medical care, such as a vacation or a new shoe that your eyes have created.

Perception is another process that you can use to manage that stress as you prepare to take it upon yourself. This cocktail in the refrigerator or chocolate bar that you have been wanting for a while will make you feel better for a while, not helping you with your goals on the beach.

Part of life

Habits are a fundamental part of daily life. It's what allows us to do more than one thing at the same time, such as driving and having a conversation. Our habits and how we break them are individual to us. Whilst we often form them without realizing it, we do have the control and power to change them.

How do habits form?

Each character begins with a structure similar to the brain "called the loop." The circle has a cue or definition, a common and rewarding function. Cue/trigger tells our brain to switch to automatic mode. This can be, for example, that when you stand or prepare a cup of coffee, you are always up for a cigarette. This behavior was noted by neuroscientists in the basal ganglia of the brain. Smoking will become a practice that no real decision can be made. The reward comes from enjoying the character, whether it is a positive attitude or a bad attitude.

How to Break Bad Habits

It is easy to think of behaviors that fall into the black and white category - good training, at a disadvantage. But behavior is also an extension of our ability to control them: some small, such as take off your shoes and place them in the center of the room each night; others are hot-headed, like having dinner on TV or drinking too much when you go to a party; and then those who are strong and addicted - like to smoke.

Emotions are difficult to destroy because they are so deep in our minds by repetition. And if you make fun of them - as you do with porn or porn - there is also a place for entertainment in the middle of gas.

But behavior is also a pattern of behavior and it is the explosion of patterns that is the key to self-blame. Usually, there is a clear definition to start the model. Sometimes the results can be emotional - thirst, smoke or nail stress. In other situations, the true definition is simply the environment and environment of the friend: you see the TV and the chair when you enter the door, and now your brain connects. Dinner in front of the TV on the couch not far away. Usually, it is a combination of both - the combination of the debate and the surrounding community leads to increased alcohol consumption.

But these models are often wrapped in larger versions. Here, once you arrive at the door after work, take off your shoes, grab a beer, sit in front of the TV with dinner without much thought, just like your morning routine. Working will allow you to go outside and chat when you all have your morning cigarette.

Overall, modern-day behavior has been modified and improved. They prevent us from getting behind the wheel of our daily lives by making the decision less than a day, giving us more freedom to think about other things. The disadvantage of modern models is that these models end up in a bad place rather than in a good column.

Find the root cause

Your bad habits have not improved themselves. They are caused by years of redundancy and as a result, are not easy to eliminate. This is the reason why most people who try to lose weight by limiting weight loss have a good weight loss. Trying to change your behavior at night is a good way to get frustrated and stop. Before doing anything else, do spirits search to find out what causes your bad habits? For example:

• Do you eat bacon or sweets because they provide comfort on a stressful day?

• Do you smoke because they relax your muscles?

• Does TV distract you from the problems you face in the real world?

The first step to breaking a bad habit is to understand why it happened.

You don't eliminate a bad habit, you replace it

What habits you have - good or bad - are the reason in your life. In the process, these habits give you a good deal, even if they do something other than good for you.

Sometimes the benefits are biological, like smoking or using drugs. Sometimes it's emotional, like living in a relationship that's not good for you. In many cases, your negative emotions are easily overcome with anxiety. For example, at the nail, pull on your hair, cup your feet, or tighten your chin.

These "benefits" or reasons also add to bad practices.

For example, if you open your e-mail in the box when you open your computer, you will concentrate. At the same time, look at all the emails that destroy your invention, redistribute your color and overwhelm you with anxiety. But it prevents you from thinking that you miss something. And so do it again.

Because bad habits bring benefits to your life, it is difficult to eliminate them easily. (That's why simple instructions like "Just Stop It" don't work.)

Instead, you need to replace bad habits with new habits that give similar results.

For example, if you smoke during stress, it is a bad plan to quit in this case. Instead, you need to come up with another way to deal with stress and absorb this new behavior instead of smoking.

In other words, habits are focused on special needs in your life. And as a result, it is better to replace your unhealthy habits with healthy habits that respond to similar needs. If you hope to exclude bad practices without replacing them, you will have some unmet expectations and it can be difficult to stick to practices like "just don't do it." him "for a very long time,

Cut out as many triggers as possible

If you smoke while you're drinking, don't go to the cafeteria. If you eat biscuits at home, throw it away. When you first sit down on the couch and pick up the remote TV, you hide it in a cup in another room. Make it easy to break bad habits by avoiding what is causing them.

At times your surroundings make it difficult for your bad habits and heavy-handed behaviors. Change your environment and you can change the outcome.

Join others

How often do you try to eat private food? Or maybe you "quit" but you keep it to yourself? (That way no one sees you fail, right?)

Replace, connect with one person and succeed together. Both of you can share responsibility and congratulate your winners together. Knowing what others want you to do better is valuable support.

Surround yourself with people who live the way you want to live

You don't need to ditch your old friends, but don't underestimate the power of finding some new ones.

Visualize yourself succeeding

See yourself throwing away the cigarettes or buying healthy food or waking up early. Whatever the bad habit is that you are looking to break, visualize yourself crushing it, smiling, and enjoying your success. See yourself building a new identity.

You don't need to be someone else; you just need to return to the old you

So often we feel that we need to become new people to overcome bad habits. The fact is that you already have it in yourself to be someone who does not have your bad habits. It's not like you've had these bad habits for the rest of your life. You do not have to quit smoking. You just have to become a non-smoker again. You don't have to turn yourself into a healthy person; you just have to be good. Even though it has been for many years, you have already lived without this bad habit, which means you can do it again.

Track to Reinforce Your Determination

This is not a way to get rid of bad behavior, but it is always helpful to eliminate the behavior. In the case of Small Steps, this is made clear. If you want to limit yourself to a few cigarettes, you need to keep track of their numbers, right?

It is also a good idea to keep track of the pros and cons when it comes to your behavior. Most importantly, monitoring is about finding out that you did not use your bad habits in the day. However, you can use tracking even when you are out of cold turkey, and it shows the strongest of these tools. When you put away your bad habits, start counting down the days without your addiction. And you create a series that inspires you to keep going.

If you're clean for a day and not even a year has passed, it's bliss. Day two in a chain looks like an event worth celebrating. Then comes the first week, the first month, 100 days in a row, the first year. This history will give you a glimpse of accomplishment, no matter what you do. That's the goal of the exercise, isn't it? Also, supervision works the only way to build your ethos. It focuses your mind on the things that matter and motivates you to move on.

It also has negative keywords that help you identify dangerous and dirty places. In the beginning, it is necessary to identify your fertilizer. then, it will help to see if you have completed a new job or how much you avoided or rebuilt your bad habits.

What does psychology say?

Decide that you want to change and convince yourself that you can

You can only change what you want to change. In all theories of change, the importance of cooperation is expressed as a necessary first step. If you do not see a problem, you will not work to change your behavior. The more honest you are with the way your behavior goes along with it, the more likely you are to stay in shape. For example, you might want to keep track of your bad habits — how often you are late, smoking, smoking, lying or drinking too much. To motivate yourself, open dialogue with people in your area can prove invaluable. People interested in you can give you the mirror you want to see your behavior as problematic as it is.

Believe in yourself that you can achieve your goals change as soon as you have decided that you want to make a change. You need to strengthen your sense of self or believe that you can achieve what you want. Seeing how others make changes are inspiring, but you must feel like you have what it takes to make those changes for yourself. As you go through steps 2 through 4, you increase your self-efficacy and increase your chances of success.

Gain insight on what's causing the habit

Once you have found out the inner thoughts and emotions that are driving you at the wrong time, you will go a long way in changing them.

Pay close attention to situations in which you engage in unhealthy behaviors. When it is late, you have to try to control the lives of others by scheduling what you (not them) want to meet. It's also possible that your behavior may come from a type of self-referential need, or from what psychoanalysts might call "negative behavior." Unbeknownst to you, are you trying to succeed in your own life because you feel you are not worth living in a good life? Are you leaving a healthy lifestyle because you feel your body is not supposed to be well? Is your dependence necessary to some extent by the need for you to succeed or shorten your life?

Internalizing disorders can be associated with a distraction from specialized knowledge. Everyone responds to promotions - gifts that strengthen our character. Some bad habits just feel good, so we keep repeating them. They can also cause us other problems, such as anxiety, temporary loss, and these rescues as other supports. Success equals the mix. If your friends complain, if you are too late, are arrogant, or are in a bad relationship, you have no reason to change. Other people's behaviors can lead to bad habits. You are late for the meeting, and everyone strives to tell you what you missed. Now you get some color for your movie star, as well as a movie.

By discovering the cause of the behavior, you can determine how to adjust the outcome of your behavior. Use rewards that reinforce bad behaviors (caring, happy) and then use them to reward you for the behavior you want to achieve. Do you like being late? Find other ways to find out. Isn't this fried delicious? Find ways to enjoy healthy eating.

Set reasonable goals at first

Their disadvantages took years to establish themselves. They will not be disposed of immediately. Choose a real-time strategy that works for you based on goals you believe you can achieve. Overcoming your sedentary life is a good example of how. First, do not assume that you can easily transition from zero training days a week to seven. You will have failures and then use your failures to prove you cannot. Instead, create opportunities for access to the gym or a challenge that fits easily into your existing schedule. Start slowly (two or three times a week) and continue slowly until you reach a level that is reflective of your age, gender, and family history.

When it comes to behaviors such as time delays, it can be difficult to achieve the ultimate goal without being one step too late. If you usually meet your appointment 20 or 30 minutes late, set the goal of being "only" 10 minutes late (this also affects others, but less often). It is unlikely that you can make any immediate changes if this practice is deeply supported by others and is caused by some personalities. It is a good start to halve the extension.

Measure your progress and don't be discouraged by occasional slips

As you reach your end goal, you need to recognize that you have accomplished the worthy goals you set for the first step. This means you have to keep a journal or journal. For example, you can benefit from the training and management of online storage services, which also enables you to make adjustments to your data. There are certainly "apps for it" that will allow you to easily manage your recording and be able to support yourself.

If you have a long delay, you should put it on your calendar (well or in writing) when you visit your meeting or relationship, or when you have submitted your assignments. See which time is closer and closer to the timeline.

Your conversion will be increased, in part, by the gift you receive from your new habit. But even those who are motivated and determined to change can sometimes do so again. If you use this document as proof "you can't change it, you can't change it. Instead, find out why you are losing. Maybe your energy system doesn't work, and well the pressure of getting used to the behavior is greater than the pain of the change. Remember these situations in your journal, but if they continue to happen you need to play around with your currency. Sorry.

Seek additional support if your habits are proving harder to change

One of the best ways to build your interior is to look outside for support. If you have trouble changing those on your own, reach out to your friends, family, or maybe your supervisors. A group exercise can be more motivating than going out on your own.

Supportive programs such as Alcoholics Anonymous and Weightlifting have been created on the assumption that it is difficult to go alone, which is why these are so important in their approach.

Intrenched or unchanged conditions may, therefore, require psychotherapy. If you are eager to reach out to a mental health professional, be sure to spend time, money, or simply not, you may be surprised to find out about mental health treatment as evidence. New psychotherapy is shorter and focuses more on new mental models. Needing help does not mean you have failed. It just means a change to the need for more help than you need.

Some bad habits you need to kill to be more successful

Kill your habit of checking social media during the workday

Social media platforms are masters in keeping you there. Getting lost on Facebook can be fun, but a struggle during the day - especially if you are trying to make that presentation available to your investors.

Now we are talking about the topic, shutting down notifications on your phone too. You can check your snapshots during the break.

Kill your habit of thinking it's all about you

Your frowning boss isn't conspiring to fire you, as much as the cashier isn't giggling about your tie. They're thinking about themselves, and their problems. Not you. I promise.

It's not about you. So cut it out. Run-on that assumption when dealing with every human interaction in your life, and you'll be much happier.

Kill your habit of multitasking

Science tells us that only 2 percent of us can do many things. So don't try it. Instead, try the following: If you try to remove something from your directory, you will be able to close all browsers and apps on your screen, except the ones you want.

Otherwise, you will receive notifications for LinkedIn questions, Facebook Live posts, and tweets. So shut down everything except the program you want and finally get it done.

Kill your habit of comparing yourself with everyone

You will never win this game. There will always be someone smarter, better looking, richer, and (seemingly) happier. Always. Focus on yourself, your mindset, your health, the state of your being, and you'll win.

Kill your habit of complaining

It's just not worth it. Be aware of the words that come out of your mouth. They affect you and the people around you.

Speak of good things, and more good things happen. Speak of negative things, and more negative things happen.

Kill your habit of wasting time with negative people

If they don't love and support you, get rid of them. You don't have to shout, kick, and scream. Just stop being available to them. They won't notice. They're too self-centered to care.

Kill your habit of taking or organizing long and unnecessary meetings

Small talk means a lot of things. We are all adults. Join in the conversation, do what you have to do, and do it. You can also improve relationships, have fun and make meetings more enjoyable.

Try this at your next meeting. Set a goal. As you enter the process, enter the room and have everyone share the following:

• What they work for.

• What they have accomplished.

• What they are doing that they are working on.

It works. You save about half an hour depending on your meeting time.

Kill your habit of saying yes

You may think you don't have enough time. You do. You just spend your time doing the wrong things.

Kill your habit of self-loathing thoughts and beliefs

Enough, you are good at what you do. You have it in you. If you can't say that voice in your head, start with a mental exercise. If you want instant success to be successful, list three things you want to change this year. Go straight; I will wait.

Congratulations. You made the first category. Think low endorphin in your brain? That is what you are looking for. Remember that and you break that behavior and create new ones. The attitude you make is true. Go - make stuff.

Kill your habit of sitting

Get off your backside. Run, exercise, move. But stop sitting. Oh, and get a standing desk while you're at it.

Kill your habit of underachieving

You're better than this. You have more in you, and you're not getting any younger. Start that business. Resign from that horrible job. Do it now. The only thing stopping you is you. Not your family, not your bank account.

Kill your habit of bragging about your resolutions before they happen

Your brain thinks you've accomplished them when you announce them to the world. Stop that.

Kill your habit of creating excuses

While you're at it, kill the habit of creating reasons. They're just excusing with lipstick on.

Kill your habit of reality TV, celebrity gossip, etc.

You're an adult; this shouldn't be a part of your entertainment. It's junk food for your brain. Feels great at first, but there is always a negative mental consequence.

Kill your habit of obsessing over doomsday scenarios

It's good to have some healthy skepticism, but pessimists don't change the world, motivate people, or come up with innovative ideas. They only bring the people around them down.

Kill your habit of obsessing over things outside of your control

Focus your time, energy, and resources on improving yourself. You can control everything you put in your body, think about, and do. Master yourself and become ruler of your universe.

Kill your habit of making sure everything is perfect

It isn't happening. This is just a complicated form of procrastination. This is a deeper manifestation of your fear. Get out of your way, and let it rip.

Chapter 7

Benefits and Importance of Good Habits

Leadership makes your life far beyond your imagination. Emotions are strong. Our brains hold them to exclusion from others - including decision making. More than 40 percent of what you do every day is not a decision but a habit. Attitude is not only important. They become stronger over time and become more and more automatic. So make sure you are right! Attitudes are strong because they affect the brain's appetite: a self-efficacy that results in the release of "cravings" of drugs in the brain.

Part of being healthy is replacing your new knowledge, healthy diet, exercise plan, or inspiration for a daily routine. Educators, leaders, doctors, life counselors and almost everyone else emphasize the importance of developing a positive attitude, but have you ever wondered why how leadership is important?

If you want to make a marathon run, you can't just take part in the first marathon your city has. It may take months or years to qualify for the marathon. The first step to achieving the goal is a daily practice. If you want to get a good job, you need to learn the daily habits of finding a job. If you want to be able to lift 300 pounds, you need to start a daily weight training program.

Almost everyone understands that there is a reason for having good rules and behaviors. After all, parents often start early to teach positive and positive words to their children. They know that they give their children the rewards that affect their relationships, education and ultimately career.

Throughout their lives, people are subject to the rule of law and punished if they ignore them. Schools have set rules that dictate what students and teachers should do. Workbooks are all rules of conduct and show respect for employees.

Most people will feel better by exercising regularly. Living energy is not only unhealthy but can also make us weak and tired at short sightings, which in the long run also have negative side effects. Children also need exercise to grow and develop.

The health habits taught at an early age are more and more reserved in our lives. Parents and schools should help children develop healthy habits and active lives. Studies show that overweight, obese children are more likely to be obese than adults, with weight problems increasing with age. By adding weight, children are exposed to certain health problems, including high blood pressure, heart disease, diabetes and certain types of cancer. Parents value their children's health by teaching them to enjoy exercise, exercise, and other forms of exercise, and encourage them to live a healthy lifestyle.

Why Have Good Manners?

Without a proper code, the community may be the sort of person whose behavior is unknown to the leader that others care about. People will say whatever is in their hearts, however. Spoon and elbows rock in restaurants and at home. The people who speak with his mouth will enjoy the guests.

Most parents do not want to make bad choices in the community, so they teach their children when they are young and begin to say "please" and "thank you". They encourage their children to show off their toys and not to be selfish, and as they grow older, they come to certain behaviors, such as: for example, how to teach others to correctly and how to make the first impression.

Social

Most people remember that when they were children, they obeyed the instructions before going home. Whether they were shopping in the grocery store or going to a friend for dinner, their parents made a long list of things to expect.

At the moment it looks superfluous. But as soon as they grow up and have them have their children, they understand why they are doing it now. As adults, many of us still care about life. Failure to abide by the code of conduct will result in the removal of our guests and people in other ways when they see us coming.

Professional

There is some expectation of how a business should behave in a business environment. If you follow the law, you will find that someone knows what you are talking about. However, if you don't, you may have to laugh and maybe even ignore it. In the long run, a bad attitude in the workplace can cause you to progress, or even worse, your job.

Advantages of Good Habits

As humans, we only have a limited number of goals. The problem is when you start something new or try to get into a routine that you are not used to. One study also shows that strength can be just as important as IQ when it comes to one person or achievement. Who do you think will do more in their lives? Some middle-aged intellectual who tends to get up and walk? Or a trivial person does not think about care. If you are a competitor, don't worry. After reading this article you will discover the benefits of good practices.

So you can expect to achieve the good in your life when you are not good.

Why you should create a practice

You develop the attitude. Your energy is going to go away very quickly because you need a lot of brainpower to start something new. While it takes energy to start a behavior at the beginning, once you have developed the habit, it will require less energy from your brain and less time and effort to sustain it. This study of mice found that when a mouse was placed in a labyrinth with chocolate hidden somewhere inside it, it would take a lot of brain cells to find the chocolate thing first, but as they were conducted several experiments, the amount of brain activity increased the brain of the rats decreased significantly. As you can see, the benefits of good conduct far outweigh the benefits of energy.

Habits VS Willpower

Compared to the soft, the quality of the look is good. Many things in life can hinder your goals or throw you off course. Once you have acquired the habit, you are slowly struggling with yourself to repay the usual amount of money you have set up.

If you spend money on chewing, drinking too much, eating poorly or not exercising at all; that is just as much a character as the other side of the spectrum. Once you know this you can begin to change your negative habits into positive ones.

When you are trying to reach a goal, it can be a solid step. 1lb a week, and you are not hitting a small goal you will become frustrated, frustrated and give up trying to achieve the same goal. However, if you don't want to get started in eating, then you can do it to rest assured that you are a category closer to the desired benefits.

Lots of attitudes

Imagine doing four activities every day that you do not want to do. For example, imagine you have 4 AM. Follow a 10 hour fast, and then when you eat, you can only eat fried chicken and broccoli. Lastly, to top it all off you go to the gym 2 hours daily. I don't know about you but to me, that sounds like a scary day. The amount of money I can expect from that every day is far greater than I have. And most people I think about.

Think about it now if you start with only one and every day. In the end, that will become a habit and you will never think about it. Then you add another character and others. Up to this point are just a few of your time.

A Balanced Diet

A varied and balanced diet is a key factor affecting the growth and development of the body and mind.

Breakfast is one of the most important foods for children because it gives them the energy they need for a day out. So let's take a look at what a healthy breakfast should be.

What kind of breakfast should it have? Foods that contain milk (milk, yogurt, cream cheese, etc.), carbohydrates (grain, cakes, etc.) and fruits (fresh, thin fruits, juices, etc.) things).

In general, the following nutritional guidelines are recommended for children to achieve good nutrition:

1. More fruits and vegetables.

2. Lack of protein.

3. Multiple bowls of cereal.

4. Less on fast food.

Sports

A well-fed baby has more energy to learn and improve body function. Sport is important for children to grow up happy and healthy. Children today are used to spending time in front of the screen when their body needs activity. That's why we have to work extra hard to make sure our kids are active and spend more time outdoors.

Controls weight

A healthy diet and regular exercise can help you lose weight and lose weight. According to the Mayo Clinic, it is important to work out physically to achieve your weight loss goals. Even if you do not lose weight, regular exercise can improve heart health, strengthen your immune system, and improve your energy levels.

Schedule at least 150 minutes of weekly physical activity. If you are not able to spend a lot of time during this exercise, find the easiest way to make it your daily routine. For example, try to walk instead of driving, climbing the elevator, or walking while you're on the phone.

Weight loss, the unknowns also help control body weight. If you start the day with a good breakfast, make sure you don't get hungry later. This will allow you to run before lunch to get a quick meal.

Also, skip breakfast may raise blood sugar, which results in excess fat. Add at least five servings of fruits and vegetables a day to your diet. These low-calorie and nutritious diets help maintain weight. Limit the consumption of sugary drinks such as soda and fruit juices and select lean meats such as fish and turkey.

Improve the mood

The positive effects on your body also pay off in your mind. The physical activity led to the production of endorphins. Endorphins are chemicals in the brain that make you feel better and relaxed. Ability to eat and exercise can lead to better regulation. You will feel better on your face, which can improve your self-confidence and self-confidence. The short-term effects of exercise include less stress and improved skills.

It is not the diet and exercise that make you feel better. Another health factor that enhances the brain is the relationship. Even if you volunteer, join the club and participate in live performances, teamwork can improve mental and emotional health by keeping your mind active and stimulating your serotonin levels are equal. Do not isolate yourself. Make time, if not every day, time with your family or friends. When there is a distance between you and your loved one, technology allows you to connect. Pick up the phone or start a video chat.

Combats diseases

Good health prevents certain health problems such as heart disease, stroke, and high blood pressure. If you take care of yourself, you can keep your cholesterol and blood pressure in a safe place. As a result, your blood flow improves and decreases the risk of cardiovascular disease.

Exercise can help you deal with a variety of health problems, including:

• High blood pressure

• diabetes

• depression

• some types of cancer

• Arthritis

Make sure you plan a physical exam every year. Your doctor will check your weight, heart rate, and blood pressure, as well as urine and blood tests. This appointment can say a lot about your health. You must consult with your doctor and listen to recommendations to improve your health.

Boosts energy

We all have expectations after eating too much unhealthy food. When you eat well, your body gets the fuel it needs to maintain your energy. Healthy eating includes:

• whole meal

- Muscles

- Low-fat dairy products

- fruits

- vegetables

Regular physical activity also improves muscle strength and endurance, giving you more energy, says the Mayo Clinic Sport to carry oxygen and nutrients to your tissues and to strengthens your cardiovascular system, making you stronger for your daily tasks. It can also boost energy by promoting good sleep. This will help you sleep faster and sleep better.

Insufficient sleep can trigger a variety of problems

In addition to feeling tired and tired, you may feel irritable and irritable if you don't get enough sleep. Besides, poor sleep can play a role in preventing high blood pressure, diabetes and heart disease, as well as lowering your life expectancy. To improve sleep, stick to the time you wake up and go to bed at the same time every night. Reduce your consumption of foods that contain caffeine, limit sleep and create a comfortable sleeping space. Turn off the lights and TV and keep the coolant down.

Being good at home creates the conditions for good behavior

Your kids will be observing how you handle different situations. Therefore, parents need to be good role models. If you are polite and consistent with them and follow the guidelines of appropriate behavior, you have several similar practices.

The character of knowledge is accepted

Professional skills are important, but you don't just need to figure out how to work. Following the rules at work will help you gain respect and the potential for increased support and promotion.

Customer-friendly sales increase

Show your positive attitude to your customers by saying goodbye to them and allowing them to express their needs, and you can earn their business in the future.

Being polite to your friends will keep them calling

When your friends know you care enough to have good manners with them, they are more likely to include you in activities and events.

Romantic relationships are stronger when couples respect each other

Men and women who are polite and disrespectful of themselves are much easier than those who are selfish.

If you treat others with respect, they want to treat you better

Whether you need food assistance or have a complaint about a product: If you teach good behavior, business partners want to work with you. Keeping the door open for a young mother or adult can make their day better. Smile at someone, and that can be brilliant in his or her time.

Good driving can help prevent accidents

Anger is never good for a person. Make sure that all drivers are wrong. It is up to you to control emotions and avoid accidents by knowing everything around you when you are behind the wheel.

Others listen when you give them time to speak

Being a good conversational partner means more than knowing the right words or words at all times. The person you are talking to may think it is important that you breathe and hear what he or she says.

Good leadership will keep your name on the guestlist

If you sign up if you say you're going to do it, be polite to others, have a great dinner table, know when to go, and thank your landlord for the invitation, there's well that you are invited back to buy.

Emotions form the basis for life

As practices become your norm, the habits you follow determine the tone for your life. If you have a habit of welcoming your children with joy, you will become a happier person. If you have a habit of eating vegetables with every meal, you become a healthier person.

Habits are step one of your life plan

When you have goals in life, it is not the goals itself that will help you realize your dreams, but the habits you develop and follow as you try to reach them. Attributes are the easiest building to reach for a goal or a complete plan.

Habit removes wasted time

As humans, we love to waste a lot of time. Most of us don't want to do anything difficult or difficult. However, when we develop good habits, we do better and this reduces waste time.

Attitude can change the motivation

We all have days when we just don't want to work, play or eat well. But when these things are a habit, they become second nature and we do them without thinking. If a healthy diet is going to become a habit, even if you are eating a cake today, you probably will not eat and make healthy choices tomorrow.

Don't lose the cart

When you start a new habit, small things can take away your effort before they become a habit. You can prevent this by finding out why you want to stop the process and cancel the transaction. You may also find easy ways for acquaintances in your new habits. It can be as simple as changing sports clothes as soon as you step in the door or remove unwanted food.

Establishing a foundation for healthy eating will help you from now on in the future. This is not an impossible task and a few simple ideas can affect the process a lot.

How do we instill these habits in the young generation?

We teach by example. Teaching healthy practices to our children will shorten and prolong life for the better and as a result, healthier life for adults. We can make a healthy life by practicing ... one or two habits at the same time. It is not recommended to report any changes that are needed immediately. Instead, move on to the following as soon as they get one or two strokes.

Illustrated by examples, shows activities such as walking, eating well or washing hands before eating, etc. Even though this cultural engagement teaches children that this practice is not a punishment, but an act of healthy living that we all do together.

Attributes that we want to share, do not intimidate, reinforce negative phrases like "Don't do that, don't eat them ..." and replace them with similar benefits. like "Then, let's go on a walk ..." Dessert Foods with your kids enjoy and talk about meal planning and sharing reasons to choose food.

Exercise for children

Continuous education strengthens, improves coordination and improves overall health. Most people are aware of the physical benefits of the game, but judgment does not end there. Physical activity helps to reduce stress, reduce stress and eliminate stress. Children who are allowed to use electronic devices are better able to control their behavior in school and often improve their performance compared to those who do not. Even young children can still manage to keep up with the opportunity to play, and the connection between play and living remains with them throughout their lives. Although the amount of time children spend watching TV or playing video games is not necessarily harmful, the majority of their free playtime should be involved, including play.

Participating in sports and other recreational activities not only enhances children's physical and emotional well-being but also allows them to interact, helping them to form friendships with them. friends. Much has been learned in early childhood, with the emphasis being on the importance of being good with others. Children in the theater or playing computer games do not have many ways to improve their social skills, which puts them at a disadvantage compared to children engaged in play activities.

Childhood obesity is the most prevalent in history and poses a serious threat to the health and well-being of a generation of children in fact. This situation in children's health is dangerous, but it can be reversed. Parents are responsible for making sure that their children are well-nourished and active. Planning family trips, games, and health tips are all options that help children stay healthy and safe throughout their lives.

Many schools are dedicated to the development of all children. They provide students with many ways to be active and healthy during and after school. There are also school lunches for healthy and healthy meals throughout the day. Every student is entitled to one breakfast! Students, who are physically fit and energetic, contribute to our vision of life-planning so that all graduates can prepare for life success, post-graduation, and professional development.

Healthy habits for parents to teach children

As a parent, you pass more than genes down to your children. Kids pick up your habits too — both good and bad. Show your kids you care about them by sharing these nuggets of health advice that they'll carry with them long after you can carry them.

Make eating colorful

Eating foods in different colors is not only fun, but it also has health benefits. Help your children better understand the nutrition of rainbow trout.

It does not mean that every meal should be different. But you should try to include more fruits and vegetables of different colors in your diet. The colors range from red, blue and orange to yellow, green and white.

Don't miss breakfast

If you schedule regular meals as a kid, you can increase the likelihood that your children will develop these behaviors as they grow older. Tell them what a good breakfast is:

• He begins to exercise his mental and physical strength

• helps make it stronger

• keep chronic diseases

Harvard Medical School claims that breakfast is associated with four times the incidence of obesity. And having fiber in many breakfast portions of cereal can help reduce the risk of diabetes and heart disease. Take a look at the sugar content.

Choose a fun activity

Not all kids love sports. Some may be afraid of physical education. But once they find that you are active and find a fun sport, it will be easier to stay healthy and active. You seem to be bringing your love of this work to adulthood.

If your child has not yet seen sports, encourage them to stay involved and participate. Do their physical activities such as swimming, archery or gymnastics. You have to find something that is fun for them.

Do not use potato chips

Get yourself and your kids out in the chair and out. The Mayo Clinic reports that children watching TV more than one or two hours a day are at increased risk for health problems, including:

• Disability in the school

• behavioral problems, including emotional and social problems and attention problems

• Being overweight or overweight

• Insomnia, including sleepiness and restlessness

• limited time to play

Read every day

Developing strong reading skills is an essential component of your children's success at school and later in life. According to the study, reading helps strengthen children's self-esteem, relationships with parents and others, and success in later life.

It is recommended that you make reading the part of your child play and bedtime. Research also suggests that daily reading for children can begin at the age of 6 months. Choose books that your kids like so that they view reading as a reward rather than a chore.

Drink water, no soda

You can keep the message simple. Water is healthy. Soft drinks are unhealthy.

Even if your kids don't understand all the reasons why too much sugar is bad for them, you can help them understand the basics.

For example, sugar in soft drinks does not provide nutrients according to the American Heart Association (AHA). It also adds calories that can lead to weight problems. Water, on the other hand, is a vital resource without which man cannot live.

Look at labels (food labels, no designers).

Their children, especially teenagers and teenagers, may be interested in labels on their dresses. Show them that there is another type of label that is more important to your health: the food nutrition label.

Show children how their favorite packaged food labels contain important nutrition information.

In order not to overwhelm them, focus on some important parts of the label, e.g. for example, the amount per serving of:

• calories

• saturated fats and trans fats

• grams of sugar

Chapter 8

Good habits for a healthy and disease-free life

Who doesn't want to spend the last days of his life healthy and free of disease? We think you do! So think again, what you are feeding your body.

Your diet and exercise habits determine whether you have a long, healthy and disease-free life. To have a healthy and long life, you must have a healthy body that requires you to take care of many things and follow certain rules.

A good way to manage your health is to take care of yourself. If you want to live a healthier life and enjoy your age unaffected by a variety of shots, change your lifestyle every day, even with a few adjustments. of health can bring great benefits.

HEALTHY LIFESTYLE

A life that lowers the risk of serious illness or early death. Not all illnesses are preventable. However, many of the deaths, especially from heart disease and lung disease, can be avoided. Scientific studies have identified some behaviors that lead to morbidity and early mortality. This booklet is designed to help you change your habits and improve your health so that you and your family stay healthy and long-term.

A way of life that helps you get more out of your life. Good health is not meant to prevent illness. It also deals with physical, mental and social issues. This booklet is designed to help you make healthy choices in your life, giving you many opportunities to enjoy many aspects of your life longer.

A life that will benefit your whole family. If you choose to live a healthier life, give other family members, especially children, a better model. They also create a better environment in which to grow. By helping them find a healthy lifestyle, they contribute to their well-being and commitment to life now and in the future.

Lifestyle Diseases Are Preventable

If you take a look at the advice these false people have consistently shown, such as "unhealthy foods, just calories", you will find that some of the common diseases we face today are blocked. They are for a reason called lifestyle disorders because our lifestyle is bad for them or helpful to them.

This category includes all matters related to biological dysfunction associated with the Western diet and lifestyle. This includes overweight, type II diabetes, heart disease, high blood pressure, certain cancers, and many, many other things. If you follow the guidelines below (for the rest of your life), you can avoid these diseases and it may even reverse them if they are already beginning to improve.

Eat Healthily

Eating foods can sometimes be difficult, but eating a healthy diet is a lot easier.

First of all, avoid sugar. As we know, sugar is not good for the body. Therefore, it is often one of the first points we omit from our menu, to help not only with weight loss but also for overall health. Transplants, oils, and processed foods should also be avoided.

Eat a healthy diet of meat, fish, eggs, vegetables, fruits, nuts, seeds, fats and fats. If you can resist them, dairy and some gluten-free grains are good too.

If you are overweight, the best way you can improve your health is to lose weight. Low-fat diets work well for that, although other exercises work well for some people.

The best meal plan for you is the one you can follow in the long run.

Eating less often (fasting for a while) and eating less (reducing calories) are ways to prolong your life. These are two of the most important pieces by any artist.

If you don't have a lot of suns you should consider taking a vitamin D supplement. Insufficient Vitamin D is associated with many diseases, and if you avoid it, it can make you healthier for longer. To find out whether or not you need it, ask your doctor for a blood sugar level of 25 (OH) D. Omega-3 fatty acids. If you do not eat a lot of fish or feed animals, you should consider adding fish oil. Other supplements that may help include magnesium and vitamin K2. These are often missing in new recipes.

Most of our health depends on our diet. Poor nutrition is the main cause of our illness and illness. You should keep vegetables, fish, meat, eggs, fruits, nuts and seeds in your shopping list. Eat an apple every day to keep doctors away, be patient! Eating apple is a good heart for you.

To be healthy and free from disease, you will need to eliminate certain foods from your diet. Unfortunately, junk food was out of the question; they will not be effective for your health. These foods make you fat and lazy.

Exercise Regularly

The importance of exercise cannot be underestimated. It is one of the foundations of good health. Efforts are made to improve health and prevent many diseases.

If you have a desk job, you should make sure to take at least three exercises per week. Certain tasks are more rewarding than others, but in my opinion, it is important to do something. If you like sports, go to the gym. If you like running, you should run. If you love to swim you need to swim. You get the picture.

Instead of focusing on calories, you need to improve your immune system. The calories are incredible, however, and exercise can help you lose weight in other ways. Ideally, you will do both cardio and some cardio exercises. Some sports teams and teams think about this.

It is most important to do something fun for you!

Although doing physical activity will help your body, some exercises may be better for you than others. For example, let's compare 45 minutes walking or running, swimming and biking. Bathing is a physical activity that helps your body function best. It moves the organs of the body in an efficient way that allows blood to flow to the muscles. This forces the oxygen around the various parts of your body, which improves the energy and the process of recovery.

Bike riding is also one of the best forms of cardio so you can stay fit and healthy. It is fun and fun for people of all ages. Make sure there is the right amount of pressure in place to maximize the performance of your bike. Men do not have to worry about their depression too much, but women have wide ears. Given the physical differences, it is important to choose a comfortable way to feel comfortable.

For a breakthrough, consider the Human Trainer fitness room. The gym is the perfect way to do a home fitness workout without investing in high and expensive equipment.

Sleep Well

In the western community, sleep is the most common. We seem to have a lot of work and distractions to get the sleep we need.

If you suspect that you have a disorder such as sleep apnea, which is a good fit, agree with your doctor. It can be repaired.

Some tips for improving sleep:

• Do not eat or drink at the end of the day.

• Sleep and wake up every day, including weekends, at the same time.

• Sleep in a dark room with no lighting.

• Let your light shine a few hours before bed.

• Expose yourself to the light of the morning, preferably by the sun.

• Avoid caffeine after 2-3 p.m.

• Eat a healthy diet and get regular exercise.

They must be properly compensated for all aspects of daily life. A good night's sleep helps us regain our tiredness at the end of the day. Adults need at least 6-7 hours of sleep. Poor sleep reduces your risk of depression and heart disease. Studies at Harvard Business School have found that people who sleep less than 7 hours a night may experience high blood pressure if they go to bed just an hour earlier.

Avoid stress

Like sleep, stress is something that comes with our lifestyle.

It is important to avoid unnecessary responsibilities. In other words, simplify your life as much as possible. Join and avoid delays. Meditation can be very effective in dealing with anxiety. If you are a stressful person, you should try this. As with all other things in life, eating well and exercising can be stressful.

It is important to reduce stress to get a happy life. Depression and anxiety are the strongest forces that silently kill our happiness. These cause other diseases such as sleeplessness, alcoholism, asthma and so on.

So, stay away from anything that gets you frustrated. Good thoughts. You will see many things to see in the future.

Conclusion

More than what we eat. We are what we give food! It is important to pay attention to what your body needs rather than just satisfying your needs. No one wants to suffer from a fatal illness at the end of his life. You only have one body, take care of it!

Because health costs more than wealth. Especially if you have money, but not the repair.

Healthy Habits for a Disease-Free Brain

When we think about healthy behaviors, we think about moving, eating better, working better, and spending more time doing what we love, with whom we love. For some reason, we are less focused on genetic information: the health of our brain and the important role it plays in our quality of life.

Okay, so sometimes the fog happens for the best of us - we're joking about "old times" that we can't find our keys or open the refrigerator if we are going to be ready to open. a microwave - but it can also be your brain. The man asked for good food in which he could live.

Current research highlights the important role of diet in improving brain function and brain function.

Let's start with our diet: "The damage to the brain by eating protein is unrelated to the way carbohydrates raise blood sugar, and even blood A low sugar increase can have a devastating effect on the brain."

An increase in diabetes causes brain damage caused by the blood disorders associated with all brain diseases, including Parkinson's, MS and Alzheimer's. Bottom line is that pain must be avoided at all costs to keep your brain active and active in the health system today and in the years ahead.

Cut the carbs

"Try to limit your daily diet by no more than 80 grams. Find your food to be unhealthy and sugary, for example, give your morning cup of orange juice, which will give you nine teaspoons of sugar before you even eat breakfast. Of vegetables with low carbohydrate: "An easy way to learn vegetables for their carbohydrate content is to reduce the consumption of ground-grown vegetables."

Know the glycemic index

Another good diet that is often overlooked is the glycemic index, which indicates which foods cause your diabetes to raise faster. Focus on low glycemic foods to balance your blood sugar.

Eat more fat

That is, unsaturated fats are unsalted and unchanged: olive oil, avocados, nuts, seeds, beef, and wild meat are fats that can add to your diet for safety. "Obese diet is the best food for the brain in the body, it increases fat intake, reduces carbohydrates and sugars, and creates a healthy effect on your brain that reduces harmful effects." relieve pain and give your brain a better performance. "

Nothing gluten

This protein, found in whole grains, rice, and rice, can increase by up to 40 percent in humans. Researchers believe that we are all suffering from a gluten-free diet.

Healthy

When it comes to good health, we already know that exercise is important, but research shows that even 20 minutes of exercise is associated with the development of new cells in the brain place memory and improve memory.

Tips to Stay Healthy While Growing Up

Sometimes, amid classes, studying, homework, meetings and maintaining a social life, college students forget to maintain their health. Though some students may not think they need to worry about healthy habits, developing healthy habits now will make it easier for students to stay healthy throughout their lives.

Eat Right

A healthy diet will boost students' immune systems, help them lose weight, and keep them healthy. Sometimes, finding a good restaurant or fasting restaurant can be difficult to manage in college. However, there are easy ways to customize your eating habits. Breakfast is always available. This can be difficult if you rush out the door to these 8-hour courses. However, grabbing bread or bananas keeps you from eating too much each day. Don't skip meals. Again, the typical days of college students are often nothing more than a routine, but you always have the opportunity to get healthy or have sandwiches. beautiful from the dining room. For a nighttime meal, try to do something better for your favorite food. For example, get pizza with wholemeal crust, vegetables instead of meat and low-fat cheese. Snacks are also a great way to increase your appetite throughout the day. Snacks can stop "people forgetting to eat" and those who eat comfortably. Have fruits and vegetables, fruit, pita bread or cream cheese ready to keep you from buying unhealthy snacks. Last but not least, consider these three factors when choosing food: persuasion, variety, and balance. Try to get a daily balance of dairy products, grains, fruits, vegetables, and protein.

Exercise

Activities that fit into the schedule are often difficult, but most schools are easy to keep students moving. One simple way of relocating is to the classroom. Depending on your schedule, this will make a 20 minute practice day. Most colleges have physical and physical programs. Use them for fun to move. Also, most colleges offer free or reduced-cost activities. This is an advantage that ends after graduation. Take advantage of it now.

Get enough sleep

Whether you are tempted to study All-Japan to study for a test or stay out until 3 in the morning to celebrate with friends, you should not be his character. Poor sleep can lead to brain dysfunction, tiredness, headaches, and weight loss or weight loss. College students need between seven and nine hours of sleep and this amount can improve overall health. To relax during the day, take a nap during the day, save time, keep your room dark and quiet before bed and avoid caffeine, eat before bed and eat rice to drink.

Wash your hands

While the flu season is just around the corner, hand washing can be a protection for college students who can't afford classes because of the flu. College students are always in touch with one another: from academics, living with neighbors, across campus, and it's very easy to get cold. or infection. Studies have shown that only washing your hands can prevent many illnesses. Wash your hands before eating if you touch your eyes, nose, or mouth, or if you are near other patients.

Do not smoke

Everyone has heard about the many health risks associated with smoking, and even if you smoke one at a time, you may still be at risk for diseases like pneumonia, heart disease, and pneumonia. If you would like to leave, check with your student's local health department for programs that support you.

Avoid sugary drinks and drinks

Although caffeine-containing drinks such as soda and soda can be beneficial for studying or doing homework at night, they may be harmful in the long run. The combination of caffeine and sugar in these drinks slows you down and then makes you feel bad. If you need a boost, try a diet that is high in protein and fiber.

Get a flu shot

This is one of the easiest ways to prevent the spread of cold and flu in the winter. Many colleges have influenza vaccines and tests at low prices, often under $ 25. Although it may be expensive for people on a tight budget, it would be better and cheaper, in the long run, to get the shot now than to get the flu later.

Drink plenty of water

If you drink enough water, you can concentrate better and avoid physical activity. It also rejuvenates your body and boosts your energy throughout the day. Always choose to have water and non-alcoholic beverages with you when you go to school. Buy water bottles and reusable water bottles from recycled plastic to cut costs.

Relax

College students are often overwhelmed with classes and exams, but rest time is key to staying healthy. Stress can cause many problems, and being overweight can also affect your health. The easiest way to relax is to make time and relax. Also take time to play with friends and reduce stress by reading a book, watching your favorite TV show or choosing entertainment.

Sunscreen and avoid drying

In less than six months in the spring, thousands of students will be at the beach. Make sure you protect yourself, even if it is not bad to spend some time in the sun. Take daily sunscreen, especially if you know you are in the sun, and reapply the sunscreen every two or three hours to make sure you are protected. Also, avoid sunbeds at any cost. Even if you want a long-lasting summer tan, the risk of skin is just not worth it. With all the oil-free sunsets available today, you can still let your summer go by without harming yourself.

Tips for a longer life

Regardless of your age, you can make any changes that affect how long you live, how you feel and how you feel for years to come. The actions you can take to make your life longer and happier are simple:

1. Do not smoke.

2. Enjoy daily physical and mental exercise.

3. Eat a healthy diet rich in foods, vegetables, and fruits, and replace fats with trans fats and trans fats.

4. Take a multivitamin daily and make sure you have adequate calcium and vitamin.

5. Maintain healthy body weight.

6. Feel the spirit. Learn more and try new things.

7. Build community relationships.

8. Follows the analytical and analytical models.

9. Use floss, brushes, and dentists regularly.

10. Ask your doctor if you can help manage long-term side effects such as high blood pressure, osteoporosis or high blood pressure.

Smoking: An enemy of longevity

If you want to live a long, healthy life, make sure you do not smoke. Smoking causes heart disease, stroke, emphysema and other diseases like diabetes. It makes breathing difficult while exercising and can increase the enjoyment of the game. It also seems to hurt memory.

The news got better. People who quit smoking can do some, if not all, of the damage. After a smoker has quit, the risk of heart disease begins in less than a few months, and in five years it will look like someone who has never smoked. According to one study, the risk of stroke fell on non-smokers in two to four years after quitting smoking. The cancer death rate is also decreasing each year after the cessation. At any age, discontinuation works to reduce the risk of death from cancer. However, this decline is most pronounced in people who have left before the age of 50.

Eating and aging: An increase

Many studies show that eating well can improve your life and improve your health. Studies show that a healthy diet can prevent diseases that make people sicker as they age, such as heart disease, high blood pressure, cancer, and cataracts.

There is no shortage of new and emerging dietary advice. Stick to the basics with broader changes, such as B. reducing muscle; eat more vegetables, fruits, and whole grains; and create a healthy balance between calories and calorie intake.

Choose fruits and vegetables for the benefit

Get at least five servings of fruit and vegetables a day. When you fill your plate with fruits and vegetables, choose from a solid color. For more health benefits, you should eat nine meals a day. To get there, choose soup and vegetable juice as juice. Sprinkle fruit on the cereals and select it for a snack or make a sweet touch after eating.

Choose the right fats

If possible, use monounsaturated and polyunsaturated fats. Avoid battle. Limit fat intake to less than 7% of calories and fat for 20% to 30% of calories.

If you do not have heart disease, the American Heart Association recommends eating two meals a day rich in omega-3 fatty acids, such as salmon, trout or mackerel. If you have documented coronary artery disease, take 1 gram of EPA or DHA a day from fish oil and supplements, as recommended by your doctor.

Choose high-quality carbohydrates

Choose whole grains over whole grains like white bread. Not only look at the nutritious commodities such as rice and green rice but also know less about wheat products such as barley, bulgur, kasha, and quinoa. Limit your consumption of free potatoes.

Choosing protein wisely

Introduce high protein foods such as soybeans, nuts, and grains to reduce the harmful fats found in animals. If you like to eat a variety of vegetables and eat beans and grains, you will get a full amino acid diet for the week. Stay away from protein sources with high levels of fat. Prefer fish and cut good chicken. If you eat beef, opt for less fat.

Don't cook food or make meat, poultry or fish - carcinogens are made. Cutting the fat that creates the flame on the grill can help prevent it. Spread, fry, steam or bake until the liquid is completely dissolved. However, baking is safe.

Turn the paper on for extra weight

It can be difficult to turn your face on to losing weight - or just to keep track of your current weight. The following tips may help:

Line-up support

Work with your doctor and possibly a nutritionist or trainer. Ask for help to set reasonable goals and take small actions that lead to success. Also, notify friends and relatives of your location.

Close the kitchen

Make your kitchen uninhabitable after dinner - even if you have to pull out a line of sight from the front door.

Go for small changes

Reducing from 5% to 10% of your initial weight is a beneficial goal with good health benefits, including lowering blood pressure and cholesterol and lowering blood sugar.

Eat a Healthy Diet Prepare for a slow diet and whole grains

Limit carbohydrates. Enjoy the average amount of monounsaturated and polyunsaturated fats in your diet. Reduce excess fats and avoid fats.

See the section

If you eat more calories than you burn, you will gain more weight. A half-benefit person who sports 30 minutes a day should have 15 calories of food for each pound of body weight. To lose weight a week, you must lose about 500 calories a day by exercising more and eating less.

Promote more activities

If you have weight management issues or want to lose weight, it is recommended that you exercise for 60 to 90 minutes a day with activities. You can teach in one-day workshops or short workshops for at least 10 minutes. The trail is safe to use for all. Talk to your doctor if you want to do a series of activities that will double your energy expenditure. That is, one minute of heavy work equals two minutes of active activity.

Chapter 9

Bad Habits and Bad Company

The people you use your time to bring are positive thoughts about your life, your time and your perspective on the world. You can change the look of yourself. That is why it is important to know about the company you work for.

The friends and colleagues who want you to do the right thing are the ones that support you and want you to become better. They inspire you to raise your standards and believe in yourself. If you spend time with them, you are better off than before.

There will also be other people in your life: complaining and complaining about everything from bad habits. Even if you are not involved in their wrong decision, they can cause you problems. In short, they are bad companies.

Meeting with the wrong friends can put you in a lot of trouble, even if you are not involved in their bad decisions. Other people (including your parents) often hold you accountable, which means that you will have trouble even if you have not done anything wrong. Getting rid of such people can be difficult, so it is best to just avoid them from the beginning.

Getting Rid of Existing Bad Company

Begin to distance yourself

Slowly accept your invitation to leave. If they invite you to their home, avoid it. Act as if you were ill or in an excuse.

Try one of these examples:

• "I wasn't expecting to go out today."

• "Thank you for your invitation, but I'm not comfortable today."

There are still stops in them. Continuing the relationship of friendship will only make it harder for years to end the relationship.

Make excuses for them

Get ideas that you can't see. This is helpful when they are in a bad company and you gradually want to stop with them. After all, they should start to see you and leave you alone.

Some good examples of forgiveness may be childcare, asking your parents to watch you, or even signing up for a school play and saying they spend too much time.

Try one of these examples:

• "I enjoy the offer, but tonight I have a lot of work on it."

• "I can't leave today because my parents forced me to do my job."

Try to help them if you want to stay with them

Talk to them about their behavior and explain to them why their behavior affects you. Give them information on how they can change as they prepare to hear.

Some ways you can help them is to tell them honestly how they feel about their behavior, talk to a counselor or their parents, and help them deal with some of the stress in them. The lives they will be doing or helping them find people in their lives (such as sports, church and other activities or school activities)

Try one of these examples:

• "It bothers me when you make me feel like I'm not a good friend."

• "I don't like being forced to do things I don't want to do. I hope you don't."

• "I want to help you find the right solution."

Don't be afraid to stand up for yourself

If they persist with their bad behavior and won't leave you alone, continue to resist them. But if they continue to follow you, tell them you don't want to hang out with them anymore.

Try one of these examples:

- "I don't think being friends with you is good for me right now. I think I need to take a break."

- "I feel like I need to focus on other things right now. I can't hang out with you anymore."

Choosing Better Company

Think about the kind of friends that you want

What kind of friends are you looking at? If you've planned this before, you know what to look for when you make new friends. Look for people who have the kind of personality you want in your life.

Some of the qualities that you can think of are: friendship, honesty, loyalty, intelligence, or creativity.

Think about how to tell if people have these characteristics. For example, someone who is good at school is probably smart. Someone who volunteered at a nursing home might be fine. Someone who frequently works in art education is probably creative.

Meet people through your activities

Try to make friends with people with good morals. A great place to meet such people is in your local church or ministry established by your school. People engaged in activities and the community rarely had problems.

Watch out for his behavior

Do this before hanging out with a new person. If you open your mouth in school, argue or bully others, do not go near.

Choose people with similar interests and goals

It is important to hang out with artists. The phrase "You are what you eat" can also apply to the friends of your choice. If you are out with passionate, passionate people, they too will start collaborating with you. If you spend time with people who are not interested in school or are unkind to others, these practices will affect you.

Talk to counselors

There are many people in your life (parents, teachers, counselors) who have more life experience than you and would like to advise you on how to find and keep good friends. Use their tips by talking to them and asking for their ideas. It will help!

Attracting the Right Kind of Friends

Be a nice person

If you want to attract the kind of people who will be good company, you need to be a nice person who is enjoyable to be around. Be kind to others, help those around you, and make goals for your life.

Be grateful for what you have in life and what others do for you. Everyone likes feeling appreciated. Tell others that you are thankful for them.

Make good decisions

People do not want to spend time with others who cause them problems or disturbances. Decide on your own life that there are benefits to your own life and that of your surroundings.

Before making a decision, think about what choices you want to make, the benefits you can make, and make the right and good decisions.

Good in school

If you are a teenager, others can determine what kind of person you are when you look at how you focus on school. If you are motivated and trying to succeed in your classes, this will affect who you are as a person, and it will attract others who will be good companies for you.

This is also a great sign for parents of your future friends. Sometimes parents can be trusted by a new friend. But if you succeed in school, most parents will have more confidence in you in the beginning.

Get help when you need it

Sometimes we like the wrong person because at the time we are emotionally incapable of being good friends. There are many ways to get the help you need, such as consultation/treatment, by looking after your body through diet and exercise, or simply by talking about your problems with someone you trust.

A few examples of some things you need help with before seeing good friends are drugs or alcohol, many mental health issues (such as depression), or mood problems. firewood. These are aspects of your personal life that you must work on to attract the friends you want.

If you have anxiety or want to commit suicide, call your doctor right away. Talk to your doctor or call the National Suicide Prevention Lifeline.

Types of bad companies

The parasite

This seemingly admiring person stays close beside you at every opportunity, weaving their way into your network, trying to take over your course instead of charting their own. They'll leave you feeling drained and depleted, and they can cause significant harm along the way.

The selfish one

This person makes time for you only when it's convenient for them, wants to talk only when they need someone to listen, and reaches out only when they want something. A relationship should never be one-sided, and you shouldn't waste your time with opportunists.

The one who holds grudges

This person is all but unable to forget and forgive. They hold on to their resentments and grievances, seemingly unable to focus on the positive and move ahead. Unless you never make mistakes, you can't afford a grudge-holder in your life.

The promise-breaker

This person is constantly making promises--and then constantly breaking them. They try to appease you by telling you what you want to hear and then they do what they want anyway. It's impossible to build a healthy relationship with someone you can't trust.

The judge

A judgmental person has an opinion about everyone and everything. They consider themselves to be excellent at reading the character of others, but their opinions usually tell more about them than about the person they're demeaning. In time, they'll turn on you and begin telling others about the entire fault they see in you.

The liar

Someone who is lying to you often violates your trust and does not respect your relationship. Even if they lie for self-defense or out of character, they cannot rely on their integrity or even the ability to tell something close to the truth.

The disadvantages

We all have some who complain, but when some of them are complaining, criticizing and blaming, it is easy for him or her to not cooperate with you. Nothing is too good for nonstop negativity.

The odd person

This person is jealous of you, what you do and who you are. There is a huge difference between praise and envy. They can make you feel guilty for not looking at the future of your own experiences. Jealousy is a bad form of bad behavior.

The manager

Some people are wise in their ability to make others do what they want. They may be good for you only when they need something - and if you haven't been through, you feel guilty that they can win. If you consistently do things you do not want to do to someone, you may be tempted.

The one who holds your life against you

People in your life must be willing to pause and understand you if you go wrong, and forget about all your past mistakes. No one needs to hear the piece constantly reminding him of his mistake.

Negative effects

This person wants you to make decisions that will make you uncomfortable, or pull you into a bad situation. Do not trust them with someone trying something new and helping them grow. The difference is you are shy, anxious, restless or nervous or not hearing.

The unsupportive one

People in your life need to support you just as you do. You have to take care of your goals and be happy if you succeed. Unsupported people do not seem to care or support you when you need them most. Work with people who encourage you to do important things.

Remember, you will only be like the people who surround yourself with. So be brave enough to let your abusers go.

Church and evil are not good

Individuals play an important role in the behavior, attitudes, and behaviors of adolescents. He decides how they see other people, how they think and how they behave. You as a parent can influence all of this, but the things that stay with kids over the long term are learned by race. Today, people are diverse, including the media, the community, the law, and the school. Let's take a quick look at how these factors affect the thoughts and behaviors of young people and transform them into people who eventually grow up.

The influence of the media on teens

Social media has expanded today. It is currently available in the form of movies, TV, video games, social networking platforms, radio and more. They all play a role in the success of your youth. If the latter sees the cruelty of people of all races in all its languages, they can either be kind to them or mistreat them. However, if media outlets are reporting the same victims as terrorists, they are more likely to endanger everyone in this race. This is how racism has managed to survive for so long. In some societies, there is a sense of happiness that is created exclusively through the media. Young people develop their thoughts based on what they see in the media, and their behavior is influenced by these perceptions.

The Effect of Crime in Society on Teens

Crime rates and police behavior also play an important role in influencing the behavior of young people. If kids see that this crime is happening all around them, they can admit to using it as normal and will eventually enjoy it. But it can be different if the status of environmental regulation is better. When young people see perpetrators as punishment for their crimes, they realize that injustice is punished, and therefore prohibits similar decisions. Both events are affected by people when you do not play a significant role.

The influence of school and friends on young people

Schools also play an important role in developing the attitudes and behaviors of young people. They meet all sorts of people there and in many cases, their friends decide how they grow. Good friends, careers and the public will improve children's overall performance, while bad practices can influence them. They can become addicted to drugs and alcohol, even with minor offenses.

Just because people have played a significant role in developing the attitudes, thoughts, and behaviors of your teen do not mean you are alone. They must promote the good in the community and avoid the negative effects. After all, the person your teenage daughter is growing up depends on your parenting as much as it does on people.

The Evils of Bad Company

The wise and the old forget about their children that man is the company he leads. He must be a man of good character and honesty when seen together with good, polite and intelligent men.

However, it has become an object of indifference, dubious of character, and unworthy of humanity is found in those who are loose and speak angrily. Even otherwise, proverbs contain all the details of truth. Bad people are just as contagious and spread as a good company. It spread like wildfire. He is none the better. Anyone who falls within his or her support is terminated.

In some cases, it is even worse than lizards. The bite of the serpent invites a quick death, but the wolf of the wicked man injures the man forever by the pain of a sudden loss. If you are still in school or college, you are more likely to be a bad person to bad companies than adults. Older people are aware of the consequences of bad life because of their advanced age and rich past.

But young people who regard their age as eccentrics can easily fall prey to the trick of bad people and their vices. They are marked by a thirst for protest. When they find enjoyment, they become less objective. These hypocrites painted life in front of them.

They take them slowly and shorten their lives. The result is that they are dedicated to a world of crime, exploitation, threats and other forms of violence. They start by outsmarting travelers — by, shaking their heads at a pistol or shotgun and firing them if they are not prepared to part with their earnings. The end is life behind the lines, darkness, and despair, which leads to conflict.

Sometimes teens will find friendship with human-wolf interests in sheep's clothing, made up of neglect, lack of judgment and shame.

They bring such people out of their faces with no regard for their past or past lives. They wake up too late to find out their folly, and to leave the bad friends behind.

These young people often ignore the advice of their coaches, parents, and elders. It is they who make fun of their true friends and treat them with names like "shame" or "chicken heart".

A selfish friend hurts his victims at one point or another. Like the bait, he gives his friend a cigarette, which he happily accepts. He was happy with the first move. How happy he was that he began to count his gifts in heaven and made him happy. The technology is being done today and the result is a poor soul as a smoker.

Vice President Fields gets bigger and bigger every day. The boy of the room became a tad and lost his school to spend his quality time in the movie theater or go on drugs with his new friends in a lonely place.

For the sake of change, he ignored his daily gambling lessons. He becomes an alcoholic. At the end of the day, when he was last announced in class, his parents' hopes were dashed. The coaches would not change it. With its cleverness and folly; He brought a bad name, shame, and suffering not only to himself but to everyone who wished him alone in the hopes of a family.

How to protect children from bad company

Parents are well aware of the results and can tell when their children move to the wrong place. Behavior changes, failing grades and complaints from school, etc. are some of the signs. Talk to parents whose children have problems and are accused of having children. They attributed their child bad grades and bad behavior on the impact of bad company.

Well, that's half true; again, the kid hangs with the name "gang" because he looks just like them. Other parents should call it bad for their children.

Understanding adolescent behavior

It is highly improbable that the parents 'goal is to keep them safe and protect their children from harm. On the other hand, a child likes to be with others like him. To a child, it is such an encounter. Teens go to this stage where they feel accepted and belong to a group. That's why children are so similar at this age - they listen to the same songs, wear the same songs and use the same words and behave like parents and communities think it's dangerous.

Parents need to know that they cannot influence their children and determine who their friends are. In the teenage years, children are more vulnerable when they choose their friends and are more protective when parents are denied the friendships they have. This is normal as it is part of a growth phase, part of growth. Children choose to join the group and are upset when their decision will be questioned.

In their teens, children find a way to spend time with their friends. It is a difficult time of childhood and adulthood. They strive to be independent but are still tied to the hair of their parents. At the same time, parents feel it is time for their child to set goals and to lead life. There is too much for the child, which leads to the belief that the parents do not understand him, and that his friends are his lovers.

Criticizing his peers chose not to work. They may challenge you and continue their friendship. They don't see your results from your perspective, they are judged. They think you see them as incompetent and must take the lead. His young father was at the helm of adulthood, making a name for himself by his choices. You can't tell her that her friends aren't good enough, because that will mean you question her ability. His allegations about one aspect of his life affect him personally.

As a parent, good decisions are made and facing back problems. You can't make your child dislike his friends, but here's what you can do —

No criticism of friends

Teenagers are at this stage of their lives when they start to pull off their shield to become themselves. They start making independent choices and choosing friends is one of them. They "think" that they are old and wise enough to make good decisions.

Continuing their understanding of their poor choice of friends may not be so great for them. They will protect their friends while defending their decision. They cannot make fun of their friends and hope to have a conversation, or hope they lose their friends as they please. It will not happen. They will look at your behavior as an insult and it will damage their confidence. They will be far away from you.

Make straightforward comments about the conduct

If you know that your children's friends are in trouble, the best way to treat them is to make positive statements. Address things that are displeasing to your character and that you dislike when dealing with uneducated children who are struggling because of this end. But you have to be good; to tell the truth.

Think carefully about what you don't like about your children's friends. Do not judge, but express your complaint. Talk about what happened and what happened to their friends. You can say that you know that he likes being with his friends because they are cool and nice. Stick to the products that make them "cool and very good".

They smoke, sleep, cheat, behave badly with teachers, harass, steal, neglect, and so on.

These and other practices have been found. If you include them in a conversation, your child cannot protect them. So you can make your child look at the situation from your point of view. Once done, you can add that it will turn out to be their rock when it hangs with them.

Tell your child that you don't like his or her friends ignoring their education or mistakes, and then say that you don't want them to do the same. He is wrong and you are sure, he knows it too.

Phase of denial

Your child may disagree with you and may argue that he or she is not bullying and he knows what is wrong. This is when you ask him if he knows about the behavior of his friends without acknowledging him and, if so, why he joined them.

Keep your observations simple and straightforward. And make sure you have a conversation - promote the conversation instead of continuing with the monologue. The conversation should leave a chord. The acknowledgment that those with whom they are dealing with is bad should come to the child and not be forced. Do not expect immediate changes. Friendship is not involved in this way. Take your time and connect with the speaker.

Affect restrictions

Young people can go against the pressure, and if nothing works, we can. If you find that the behavior of your child's friends does not apply to your behavior, it does not do anything to impose restrictions on your child. You decide whether or not your child is allowed to mix with them and if so, when and for how long.

Be firm in your decision making and tell your child that their friends mean bad business and that you do not allow him or her to connect with them. The child will retaliate and even rebuke you, but you stick to the ground, set rules and expectations, and let him know that he will be guilty if they do not comply. You need to take the lead and discipline it properly.

Make the punishment good; do not pay for the cost of this tour.

The final word

Kids will make mistakes; it is part of the course of life. Stand firm with them; bathe with love and understanding, but be strict if you must. Too much pampering doesn't do them any good. It is your job to guide and create it. Do it without fear of his mind - and thus no physical harm and any shame or malice. Use smart rules to discipline your child. You are very smart to do that.

Chapter 10

Successful Persons Adopt Good Habits

Attributes are central to your success - or maybe you lose. Regardless of the importance of behavior, few people know much about their work. Personality is always considered negative, such as substance abuse or gambling behavior. But there can be positive behaviors, such as being consistently athletic, giving thoughtful thoughts, thinking critically, researching topics, and starting work long before the deadline.

Behavior is something we do regularly without forgetting to think about it. It's an automatic mindset and attitude. Habits lead us to act without much effort. They make everyday life possible - for better or for worse. Many people make an effort to do bad things. Nutrition is the perfect example: it is an attempt to normalize excessive or over-eating habits. Many smokers and alcoholics want to change their behavior, and many sponsors want to help them.

Also, it has characteristics that affect learning products. For example, move on from the main tasks and time spent on email, surfing the web, or simple tasks. Positive thinking is also important. For example, it is common to pay attention to negative thoughts, which can lead to impatience.

In the classes we teach, we rarely talk about behavior. The emphasis in most classes is learning the concepts and skills and perhaps the behaviors. But what if habits are more important? Consider what is needed to become a successful filmmaker. Studies of the work of experts have shown that the key is "practice". This is an exercise in which you are focused on the role and are committed to improving the teaching of the experienced coach. In the long run, practicing the violin will do more than just learn the lesson. Thousands of rehearsals must become international artists. Developing a habit through daily practice is the most important way to learn for the sake of performance.

It is a question of which character is most relevant to student performances. It may be about writing, speaking, thinking, or exploring the mind. Choose a goal - because most classes do very little to encourage long-term behavior. Most students just do what they want: they don't improve learning. Most students work at work only during exams: they do not have good study habits. Often students just do what is necessary to achieve what is needed: they do not learn to push themselves to succeed.

These techniques will not do much for artists. They will mean practicing only on paper, just practicing before the action and not trying to guess the hardest ones. The learning habits and learning styles of students are often not the basis for being a successful person. Continually learning the skills and knowledge is more important in the long run than learning content, writing, or passing.

The same applies to those of us who work as teachers and researchers. We have spent more time teaching and analyzing behaviors that we have adopted over the years or years than just improving or replacing them. This is like a durable keyboard player but uses both hands as fingerprints to upgrade.

Once you have completed your bad habits, it is time to develop some positive habits that will put you in a position to succeed. But first, you have to decide what success means to you.

Habits to make yourself successful

Getting Motivated

Most of us believe that successful people simply stand by the effort. That they are active around the clock and have never been attacked with encouragement.

However, we see these people succeed only at the moment when they make a bold decision. That's not it.

Successful people seek as much support as they need, and everyone has different personalities to get that inspiration. Some think about an hour each morning, others listen to their favorite songs while driving to work, others stand in front of a mirror shouting their approval, and others watch the movie reinforced.

Patience is an important consideration to achieve more quickly because it enables us to achieve more in less time. Successful people know this, but also know that heartache is just the emotional thing that comes and goes. They play a role in supporting themselves in some way they know. You will never find the way and the desire to be forever, but there are hundreds of small ways to stay active all the time. Use them all!!

Spending time taking care of all areas of your life

Just too much work will not get you done. The reason is that as you become better at your job, you will move on to other areas of your life.

You need an active life in all areas of your life to support a successful career. If you don't have time for yourself, you are completely burned out. If you are unable to take care of your relationship, you will be less likely to work. If you are not healthy and fit, your body will not be able to function with a gigantic role. And if you are unhappy or feel like you have spent enough time in your faith, you may feel like you are losing some things, and it can be difficult to make the most of it.

Successful people arrange time in all areas of their lives. They make it a daily routine, some time for themselves, some time with their family, some time with their partner, some time to exercise and some to feel great every day.

This is the only reason most people are not successful. They focus so much on one area of their lives that every area is lost, and then they want to know why they are so unhappy.

Look at the most successful ones: Bill Gates, Oprah Winfrey, etc. They all cover every area of their lives, fit, energetic, spend time with their family and friends, and have time for themselves. That gives them a chance to live like this! And yes, it is very difficult to keep everything under one roof, but not everyone is successful.

Take the time to intervene

Yes, you read it right: Successful people are affected. Some even watch TV, watch video games or watch movies. All this seems to have a big impact on most of us.

The difference between successful people and everyone else is that successful people plan this time. When they spend time with the stress they cause anxiety. Maybe to distract yourself or to have fun without meaning. No matter how much time they spend, they limit their time to what they need and can set the time ahead.

Most of us start to associate ourselves with a movie or film, maybe only once on one of our favorite shows. And then, before we know it, it is 6 pm. and we see 3 seasons in one sitting.

Remember, it will never be enough if you have no idea where you want to go. Be sure to know your goals before you start doing some things, especially in situations where you can easily lose.

Tracking your habits

The most talented people follow their success through the script. You might even have a weekly graph and calculator to see how well they have done, where they have fallen, and where they can improve.

The best way to improve is to get real evidence and believe in how you use your life. You may think you have a general idea of where you are in trouble and where you can improve, but if you do not write this article correctly, you will not know really.

Do you even know how many hours a week you need to succeed? You may not even know how many hours a week there are, and how many hours you have, how you feel about your life.

Follow your habits with a habit sheet, avoid any habits you want to do in your life, and figure out how much time you spend in a day. Sure, it may be a lot of work to keep, but if you don't, you'll always keep it behind because you don't even know where you're struggling.

Let me give you an example: Let's say you sleep 7 hours a day, have 50 hours a day, and spend 3 hours a day eating, visiting the bathroom and so forth and using 3 hours a day with yourself, Friends for fun. How many extra hours during the week do you have?

If you already spend 3 hours a day on your own and another 3 hours on all warranties, you still have more than 24 hours to do whatever you want to do! That's a whole day left, even if you only need 3 hours a day to do what you want.

Track your habits, list them, compute them, and know where you spend your time without thinking you know it.

The measure of success is happiness, not in wealth

Employees today are promoted by something other than wealth, with job satisfaction, efficiency and aptitude most important. This also represents a change in the way people measure their success, as the definition in pounds and pence or dollars and cents just keeps you on track to a higher level than isn't Get excited. This can be a disadvantage. So make sure you create a clear vision for success and understand exactly what this means for you.

Challenge yourself and be tough

Without personal growth, which requires a willingness to accept and make difficult choices, one cannot succeed in life. Only by overcoming obstacles can we learn and develop life experiences. These qualities are what make us successful. By challenging yourself and making it difficult for yourself, you can also change your attitude to the potential of life.

Listen to Constructive Criticism and the Opinion of Others

While positive feedback can improve your morale and motivate you to succeed, you can respond to criticism that ultimately enables you to achieve your goals. After all, this commentary addresses the areas you need to improve rather than affirming your strengths. Your weaknesses can then be overcome by training and improvement, which makes you stronger and stronger for someone.

Learn from mistakes

While failure is seen as a masterpiece of life lessons, it is easier said than done by art through passion and despair. Of course, it needs the ability to learn the lessons we can get from any mistake and we can use them in search of future successes. By solving the problem directly and pointing out where there is an error, you can step in to ensure that an error is not repeated.

Establish morning and season

Recent studies have shown that a long sleep cycle of eight hours is the reverse of your mood swings. However, it is also important that you create a consistent sleep cycle. In this way, you become a morning person who stands every day at the same time. This improves the efficiency of your schedule and creates the opportunity to perform well. While the world is still in bed, you can take action to improve your body and mind for the day ahead.

Choose a good example

While some view the fear of failure as the main reason, the limitation on the outcome. Instead, it's best to be active and use good manners in whatever you do. Given the changes that can affect your success, you must control your thinking and take positive steps to identify opportunities.

Make a conscious effort to reach out every day

Although it is recommended to wake up one morning with responsibility and good vision, it does not mean much if you cannot commit yourself to it every day. Following your routine and pursuing your goals is key to success. Otherwise, daily stress can affect your mood. This requires a lot of urgency and energy but ultimately allows you to succeed over a longer period.

Work harder than your Competition and Those Around you

While you can only manage your efforts to achieve your goals, it's important to remember that everyone's success is determined by the people around him. For example, if you are competing with others for a specific purpose or price, you must do everything in your power and not give up the stone if you succeed. Focus is your passion for the cause because if you commit to working harder than others, you will eventually get a good result.

Make it fit for your enemy

One of the biggest obstacles to long-term success is satisfaction, which can easily come after recommendations or the achievement of short-term goals. However, you should strive to use these accomplishments as a stepping stone and devote your energy to the cause. The example of footballer Cristiano Ronaldo, who, despite his rise to become one of the best players in the world, continues the challenge of protesting the daily movement that supports the development. own.

No one fears

It is extremely difficult to succeed in the work of your choice, especially as you will not be overwhelmed to see that there are animosity and a strong focus on similar goals. However, you should not let these people hurt your side or hurt you, as this will cause you a penalty and make you feel bad for competing. Although you must always respect the competitors around you, you must remain fearless and support your ability to finally succeed.

Use your focus on paper

Believe it or not, the power of the to-do list will be in the mind. This list is usually used for short-term or daily goals. There is a timetable for someone to help them understand their progress in the process. This can give you peace of mind that you will achieve your goals and be productive at a time. If you set your long-term goals on the list, you will be motivated and motivated in difficult times.

Surround yourself with Positive and Successful Individuals

Having different and mixed friends is all well and good, but the people in your community must have the same qualities as professional and professional. If you have friends who like to distract and distract you from your work, you may end up deciding whether you want to succeed or enjoy your existing life. If you are uncomfortable with the idea of removing people from your life, ask yourself whether a true friend risks your long-term happiness by preventing you from fulfilling your destiny.

Maintain a healthy and healthy body

According to the Athletes Way, many habits of daily life can help to find the perfect balance between physical and mental fitness. Several studies show a link between the two, and it has been shown that regular exercise is important in improving brain function. So if you want to improve the energy needed to achieve personal and professional performance, a proper body image is crucial.

Invest only in the pursuit of your goals

Success may not always be the best measure of success, but it can be used to improve personal and professional development. In this sense, it is more important to spend money on improving your work or your company, than just investing in a property that simply creates the image above. Making these cost-effective decisions is the key to success as you are forced to rethink your goals and evaluate how well you accomplish them.

Ready to sacrifice

Likewise, you may be forced to make a sacrifice on your path to success, because it is not as if every worthy goal can be achieved. The so-called "law of sacrifice" simply means that you cannot accomplish everything you want without the intent to give up. Therefore, you must be willing to live the full life of the various goods and possessions to continue your work.

Ways to Encourage Good Habits in Children

Parents can help their children develop healthy habits early in life. This can take a lifetime. As a parent, you can encourage your kids to learn behaviors that can include social and behavioral issues, and help them measure some of their nutritional habits and outputs. effort. It takes time to develop a habit, so parents need to be patient with their children. Repeating a daily routine or routine helps your child break it down faster.

Be a role model

One of the best ways to be a positive influence on children is to be a good example for yourself. Your child learns by observing your daily routine and behavior. Therefore, you must tell the best of his / her absorption.

Good manners

It's never too early to find the best for kids. Encourage your child to use the words "Thank you, you are welcome and excused me". If you teach them these words when they are young, you can make them a part of their lives.

Physical Activities

Physical fitness is more than a competitive sport. This includes daily chores such as walking with the dog, gardening, playing tags, chilling and even doing household chores such as sweeping or rolling around in the car.

These days, kids spend a lot of time at home watching TV or playing video games. Children who are not physically active are at increased risk for kidney disease. Encourage your child to be active by choosing fun activities. This can be swimming, biking or just getting outdoors. Exercise as a kid becomes part of them as you grow up.

Support family gatherings

Family time is of the utmost importance for children to grow up. Schedule a time where everyone in the family can be together. Go for a walk, bike, go swimming, work in the garden or just play hide-and-seek outdoors. All will benefit from exercise and time together.

Set ground rules

As parents, you must make rules for your children. Now is the time to create activities and opportunities. Schedule a difficult time with playtime, homework and screen time. Try to keep up with changing times and not be too strict when planning time for study and play. Give yourself plenty of time to play, as exercise helps with physical and mental development.

To promote a healthy diet

The most important part of growing up is encouraging your child to eat well. Your child will behave if he or she starts early. Teach your child the importance of healthy foods and encourage reading the labels. Every family will learn what is good for their health and what they know better about nutrition. It is the attitude that helps change the attitude for life.

Reward your child

It is a good idea to reward your children with good behavior. This keeps them motivated and helps them maintain their good behavior at all times. However, one important thing here is that you do not gift your child with things like chocolate or an hour of television. Find other ways to celebrate positive behaviors. Make a great gift - a hug, a happy word, and so on.

You can reward your kids with great experiences. This will help them realize that happiness is more valuable than life on earth.

Stay Involved

No matter how busy you are during the day and workday, you need to make sure you are involved in your child's life. Make sure you are aware of the day, the type of friends and activities at school. It is a good idea to talk to your children after they get home. You will still be kept up to date on the emotional impact of your children.

Family dinner

Family meals are great for teaching your children about healthy eating. During family dinners, your children may not have to eat unhealthy foods and have regular contact with family members. It also promotes the sense of attachment within them.

Encourage reading books

Read stories from books for your child to make a difference. Good reading encourages children to behave appropriately, to follow rules of conduct, and to maintain good behavior in life. Reading habits will be crucial to your child's creativity in the long run.

Be comfortable with what you need

Encourage children to learn from their mistakes. Setting realistic goals and limits is the key to new behavior. Small steps and subtle changes can change your attitude over time. So start small and build up. As a parent, you need to know that all children learn on their own.

Children do not listen to what they cannot. Instead, tell them what they can do. Keep it funny and good. Everyone likes to be praised for their good work. Celebrate success and help children and youth improve their quality of life.

Separate Good Habits from Bad Habits

You have to be smart enough to distinguish good behavior from bad before picking up information from others. Unfortunately, reporting on bad practices is easy to find and fall within our normal practices. Good practices require care and patience. For example Early morning is one of the best practices of students. If you are a late dresser and lose time in your student life, it may be difficult to let go of the behavior in the morning and repeat the same behavior. mold early. The key to good behavior is, therefore, to be more decisive and efficient. When you start receiving gifts for your newfound personality, you realize the importance of this attitude in your life. Until then, you just have to pay attention to it as your character.

Practice makes perfect - Schedule a habit

If you do something more and more often, it will be anchored in your brain and the brain will not let you separate from this behavior. Therefore, you need to make plans to improve behavior. Make sure you force it into your normal routine until your brain gathers it for you and makes your job easier. A strong person will be more likely to learn good behavior sooner than others.

Good health leads to a better life

In general, it has a lot of personality traits, and some personality traits are particularly personal to your liking. You have to be particularly well-liked by those who have a positive impact on your life and accomplishments. For example Good nutrition is a good habit that everyone should take, as it has both long-term and long-term health benefits. On the other hand, reading research papers is a positive attitude that more than any other is about students and learners. Be sure to set up your training class to avoid distractions.

Be proactive

Another important factor for good behavior management is giving away bad habits. If you have a bad attitude, you can replace it with a good one. You can be conscious of changing your behavior and leaving no room for that in your life. For example: Try reading a book during the holidays instead of watching TV. Since you are exchanging the activities of your free time, technically you have not given up any time of your time to attend TV programs. Of course, bad habits are taken away from you every day. At the same time, you learn to refresh and time to learn.

CPSIA information can be obtained
at www.ICGtesting.com
Printed in the USA
LVHW051442300321
682937LV00019B/990